What people have s

Of

I started reading it yesterda
'amazing' read from start to finish.

DT

I have just finished your book, what a strong brave person you are! There were parts where I gasped, laughed and cried. So please you are now happy.

JB

I've just finished your book, made me laugh, cry it's fantastic Brilliant book, amazing story well done for writing it.

HR

An open, honest account of of live in a culture that is foreign to you. You laugh and cry along with Tina and her boys. The book is a well written easy read that will keep you entertained page after page. I can't wait for the next book.

CA

A brilliant book...funny, with a couple of sad bits..a very enjoyable read...

JN

What a story! Have read this all in one sitting. Was gripped from the first page. A story well told.

Amazon Reader

Please write more I loved the author's style of writing, I actually felt like I was there in Turkey when reading.

SM

I've just read your book and really enjoyed it. I couldn't wait to go to bed because I only read in bed. I was completely hooked, can't wait for the second book.

MH

Tina Hartshorne

More Tales and Travels of the Fat Bird

A Yorkshire Pudding

First published in 2020 in paperback form by:

The New Science of Fixing Things Ltd, United Kingdom.

Cover illustration by David Hartshorne

ISBN: 979 8 56170 167 2

The Stories

Dedication

This book is dedicated to all the people who read my first book and encouraged me to bring the Fat Bird out again.

Thank you all.

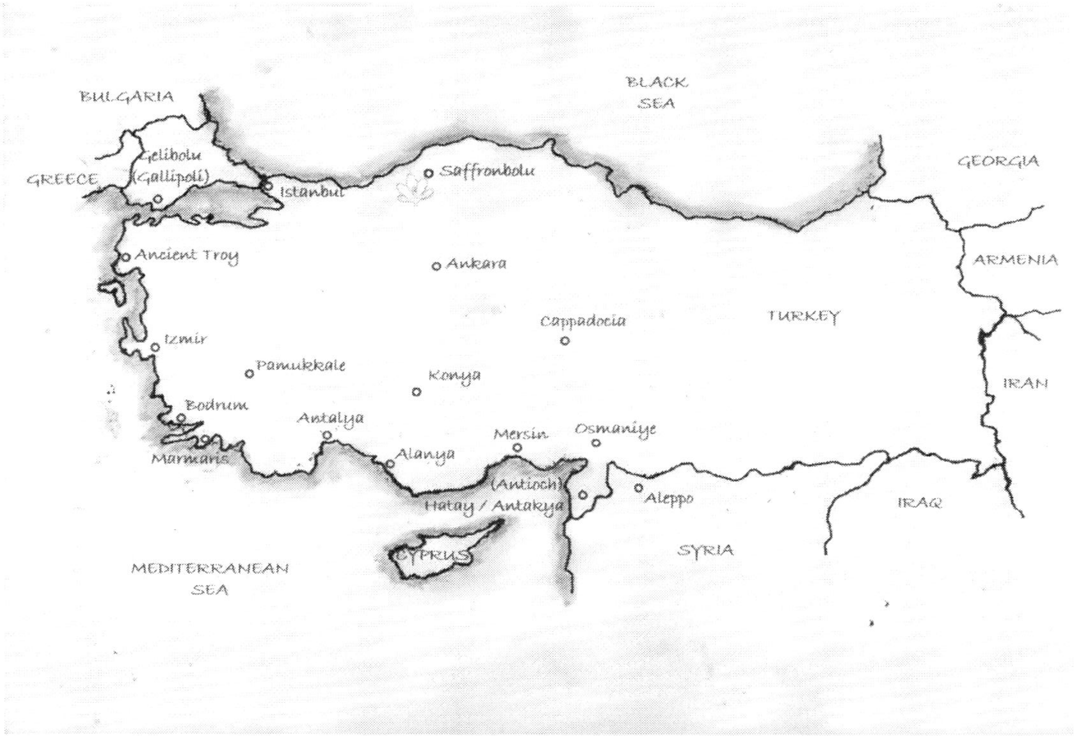
BULGARIA
BLACK SEA
GEORGIA
GREECE
Gelibolu (Gallipoli)
Istanbul
Saffronbolu
ARMENIA
Ancient Troy
Ankara
TURKEY
Cappadocia
Izmir
Pamukkale
Konya
IRAN
Bodrum
Antalya
Mersin
Osmaniye
Marmaris
Alanya
(Antioch)
Hatay / Antakya
Aleppo
IRAQ
SYRIA
CYPRUS
MEDITERRANEAN SEA

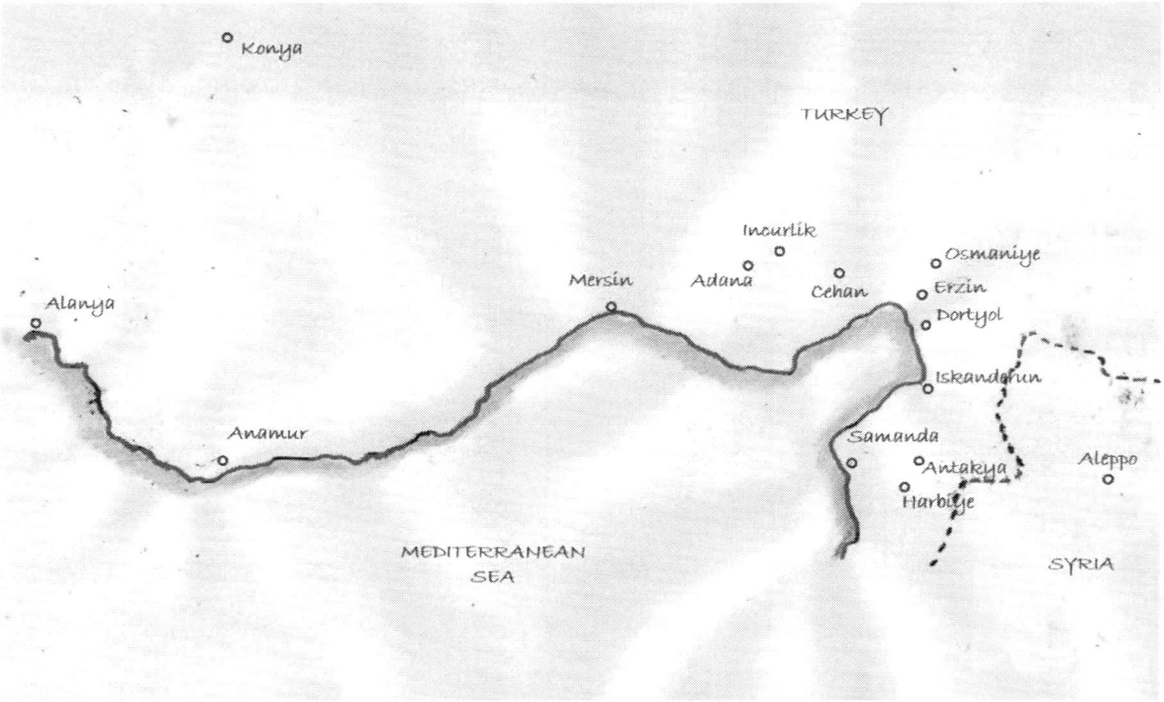
Konya
TURKEY
Incurlik
Osmaniye
Alanya
Mersin
Adana
Cehan
Erzin
Dortyol
Iskandehun
Anamur
Samanda
Antakya
Aleppo
Harbiye
MEDITERRANEAN
SEA
SYRIA

Foreword

Here we are again, another set of tales from what I consider to be my amazing life. We are all living in a strange world; everyone wearing masks, staying socially distanced were possible, and I listen and read daily of people moaning about being bored. I don't think I have ever had a day in my life when I've been bored. I also hear and read about people doing things they had never had the time to do, and I guess I'm one of those.

I decided, when the world changed, that it was my time to put to paper and actually do what I have thought about doing for years. Write my story.

I moved out to Turkey in 1998 and lived ten very unusual years there. I brought two boys up, mainly by myself, and along the way had some sad, unusual and funny times. I have already shared the skeleton of my life in 'The Amazing Life of a Fat Bird', but now I'd like to continue to share some more of my life; adventures I've had, struggles I've endured, and some more entertaining anecdotes from past and present.

I'm the daughter of a coal miner, I was brought up believing that hard work never killed anyone. I believe I have good morals, but I have a wicked sense of humour too, and over the years I have become extremely cynical. This, however, means that I see humour in lots of places that most people might not! I'd like to share some of these. I'm not always politically correct, but there is never any malice meant.

I sincerely believe that I currently have three books inside me, waiting to come to life. The first one has been out there for a few months. It was a cathartic experience to open up about a lot of my bad times. This is the second, and it is more a 'tales of' book with a travelogue thrown in. My first book was subtitled 'A slice of Turkey'. This book is subtitled 'A Yorkshire Pudding', because my Grandad, who I loved dearly used to call me his little Yorkshire Pudding, or else Bossy Boots! He died when I was young, and way before his time. My next book will be a diary of the adventures my husband and I had in New Zealand a couple of years ago. That will be subtitled 'A Kiwi Desert'. So, the set of three make a full meal.

There is no real chronological order to the stories that follow. They are a random selection of memories from my 'Amazing' file. If you were kind enough to buy my first book, and read it to the end, then you will know the characters and some of the background already. But if you haven't read my first, I have tried to make this a stand-alone book too. There are lots of short, anecdotal stories, so grab a coffee, a comfy chair and enjoy.

Cheese Man

Years ago, and I'm talking about the early days of my life in Turkey so it will be at least thirty years ago, airplane travel was slightly different to what you would recognise today. Smoking was even permitted (but only at the back). Imagine!

I lived in Turkey, and even before I did, I regularly flew with Turkish Airlines. Great airline, good staff and a comfortable plane journey, but you could see some very odd things. One brief journey I'd like to tell you was from Istanbul to Antalya. A sixty-minute flight. Simple you might think. But the problem, and I'd seen it before, was that there would sometimes be lots of elderly people travelling on this flight. I can only assume that they were travelling to meet family since they were always carrying 'things'. Lots and lots of 'things'. Sacks of fruit, boxes of all shapes and sizes, bags of aubergines, all things that could easily be bought all over Turkey. So, as I said, I just assumed that these 'things' were either gifts being delivered, or gifts given and now going home. Otherwise why else would you put yourself through the agony of carrying all these 'things'?

Maybe I should have thought better about my timing, I'd chosen to fly back to Antalya on a Sunday, I'd had a flight from Manchester earlier that day, but now the connecting flight was late evening on a Sunday. Looking back, this was clearly a bad choice, as all the elderly people with 'things' were on the same flight.

As I walked down to the plane from the gate, I was surrounded by lots of 'things'. People were being bashed and bumped by all these 'things'. Some of the elders were struggling to even carry them, they were stopping and starting every couple of metres as they walked down the aisle. One couple had a huge bag with them which was full of lots and lots of plastic style boxes containing food. Another man had a kilim (a small handmade carpet) rolled up and was carrying it onboard. Surely they would have their 'things' confiscated at the plane door? Surely they didn't expect to board the plane with this vast array and quantity of 'things'? I was starting to feel a little 'thing' envy. Maybe I should have thought ahead and bought something heavy, bulky and somewhat ridiculous that I could bring on the plane with me?

It took the longest time to get to the plane, the jetway tunnel to get to the plane door was starting to smell badly. It was that 'thing' smell. How could it not smell, when it was a cross between an allotment with a newly spread coat of manure and the day after a feast in a Bedouin tent in the desert? I was starting to imagine the horror of what an hour on a smelly plane might be like. Little did I know!

I finally reached the plane. It had been, and still was a free-for-all. Everyone was clearly trying to get their 'things' on as they were now getting heavy and uncomfortable to carry. Boarding was also so slow, as even from the plane door it was easy to see that the overhead lockers were beginning to bulge and groan under the demand for space. Elders trying to lift heavy and oddly shaped 'things' didn't work either and there was one poor steward who was so red in the face, he looked like he might burst.

I was on the plane, but now I was starting to think, did I really want to be? I shuffled along with the rest of the passengers, so slowly that I was starting to worry that we might miss our slot to take off and have to sit on the plane for an extra hour waiting for another slot. The smell was dreadful, I have no words to explain what it now smelt like. Added to the 'thing' smell was the smell of people who didn't use deodorants (back then it was incredibly expensive by UK standards and so wasn't used very much). These people had been struggling and sweating…. a lot!

My seat was about halfway back and as I approached the seat row, I saw two old men sitting in the row of three. One near the window, one in the aisle, good start as my seat was the middle. But as I got nearer, I saw the strangest thing ever….an enormous wheel of cheese sitting in my seat, and it was actually buckled in, ready to go! And I am not kidding, this is true, absolutely true! Surely, I was imagining this?

But no, when I got to my seat, there was a cheese sitting in it, seatbelt buckled, ready to go! In my best but limited Turkish, and whilst staying polite, I explained to the man sitting next to the cheese, as best as I could, that I wanted to get into my seat. Could he please move his cheese? I'd never had a conversation like that before and hopefully never will again. But much to my surprise, the old bugger refused! He absolutely refused, saying he'd paid for his ticket. But when I asked if he had bought a ticket for his cheese, he called the red-faced steward. He explained to this nice young man that he really needed this cheese not to be broken and he had paid for his ticket, as far as he was concerned he had done nothing wrong, why couldn't I be moved to another seat? The steward told him to look around, there were no empty seats, and that he needed to move the cheese quickly. The old bugger then suggested that I should stand, it was only an hour to Antalya after all. Yes, stand! Now

I know way back then that rules were much more relaxed, but stand? Then I started to lose my temper. Old or not, he was proving to be an old bastard, everyone was looking at me, but as he was still sitting down, they couldn't see him. He was clearly a misogynist and not very fond of foreigners. He was at risk of wearing his f*****g cheese as a hat. If I got kicked off as a result it really wouldn't have been a loss. The plane, this old twat and his stinky cheese were all smelling like something had died.

The steward was almost shouting at the old Cockwomble and eventually explained that he and his cheese would be taken off the flight if he didn't let me sit down. That did the trick. He reluctantly stood up and unbuckled the cheese. It really was massive, and it stank like the worse pair of stinky feet you have ever had the bad luck to meet.

Before I was able to sit down, the old Cockwomble balanced the cheese on his seat, leant forward and pulled out two big boxes which had been on the floor in front of the cheese's seat. He moved them into the aisle and let me pass.

I squeezed past him and the monster cheese which seemed to be sweating now. It was wrapped in a sort of muslin I think but it was moist. Wet? Lovely!

I sat down, wondering what the state of the seat below me was like, would I stink like the cheese when I got off the plane? I buckled my seatbelt as the old Cockwomble was still arguing with the steward, but as soon as I had finished buckling myself in, he stopped arguing and turned to me and lumped the cheese wheel on my knees!

What the f***! The Steward did shout at him now. I shouted at him now, and if I could have got a grip of the bloody thing, I would have lumped it into the aisle. He argued again saying that with his boxes he didn't have enough room for the cheese. I know where I wanted to suggest he put it, but I pointed out that he should put it on his knee. Oh yeah! Duh, misogynist and truly stupid.

He did eventually sit down, the nice young steward, pushed the boxes under the seat in front and he clearly had little space for his feet, what a shame, and then after he had buckled himself in, the steward landed the cheese onto his knee.

I am forever grateful that flight was as short as it was. I couldn't move due to the overhang of the cheese at one side and another old man on my other side, who, bless him, hadn't muttered a word. He was almost laying in his seat, so was all over the arm rest. He might even have been dead, but I had my own difficulties to deal with. The smell during the flight was worse than anything you can imagine, even to the point of making me gag occasionally.

When we arrived at Antalya, the young steward was almost instantly standing beside us. I think he realised that I was captive and that my patience might not last much longer, So he helped the Cockwomble by holding the cheese and by stopping the flood of customers who would in any second be clambering about trying to retrieve their own 'things'. The boxes were pushed out of the way, the Cockwomble stood up and the boxes, cheese and he was kept out of my way whilst I stood up and scrambled across to get into the aisle. I took my place in the queue, easing slowly forward, ready to leave the plane and as I passed the steward, he thanked me for my patience!

I drove home with the car windows open, I smelt like crap! And I never looked at a cheese wheel again in the same light!

The Lion, The Witch and the Nice Old Lady

I've always thought that the world was a small place, and this story proved it for me. I need to take you back many years, almost twenty-five. My eldest son Aslan was four, and Kaan was still a baby. We were all still living in the UK. Erkan, the boy's father, was working hard, and life was ticking pleasantly by.

I had always liked going to the theatre, and when I was working it was a great delight. I followed the Hull Truck Theatre group whenever I could, and I liked live theatre very much. I had a plan to introduce Aslan to the theatre. The local Civic Theatre were advertising that they would shortly be showing 'The Lion, The Witch and the Wardrobe'. Now this seemed like the perfect opportunity for me. My plan was, because Aslan's name would be mentioned throughout most of the play, that maybe he would stay interested and connected. At his age I was taking a chance, but I wanted to try.

I worked in an office in Doncaster at that time, so during one lunch break I walked round to the Civic Theatre to buy three tickets. I started a conversation with the lady in the box office. I explained that my son was very young, and I wanted the best seats possible, so it didn't matter which evening performance we came to. I just wanted the best seats possible. We chatted about my son, and I explained that his name was Aslan, and that I was hoping that this would keep him connected to the play. There was a man waiting at the side of the ticket box, and he was listening to the conversation. He interrupted, saying that he was the director, and he would make sure we got good seats. He then asked me about the pronunciation of Aslan, as most people say Azlan, but it's really more Asslan. He said they'd try and get the name right. The lovely woman in the box office then surprised me with three front row seats, which, she assured me, would put us in a really good place.

The evening came, and we first drove to Mum and Dad's house where we were leaving Kaan to be looked after, whilst we were at the theatre. I was excited and hoped that Aslan would firstly be able to stay still for the duration of the play, but hopefully enjoy and stay interested in it. We entered the theatre, and of course, the first thing to do was buy Aslan something to help keep him content. We bought him a box of Smarties, that normally worked.

We walked into the theatre itself, and Aslan was amazed and was looking about. When we took our seats on the front row, he was happy and becoming excited. Now, this is no word of a lie, but from the second the curtains were pulled back to the end of the show. Aslan never moved. He had a smarty halfway to his mouth when the curtains opened and I had to steer the smarty in, but he didn't touch the box again. He was enthralled, absolutely enthralled, and when the characters started saying his name, he was gone. He was loving it.

The nice lady in the box office had been spot on, as during the play Mr Tumnus the 'faun' would regularly jump from the stage and land on the floor almost in front of us. The white witch was pulled in her sleigh down the aisle and stopped at the side of us whilst performing. It was fantastic, and Aslan was in Narnia, he was truly in Narnia. When the character of Aslan came on stage, I could feel Aslan was so tense, but it was excitement, he had been taken away to another world. He didn't need to talk, I don't think he could, he was stunned and absolutely loving every second.

As the break approached, I asked if he needed the bathroom, but Aslan had changed from a enthralled statue to a chattering excited youngster, asking so many questions about everything from Mr Tumnus's lack of legs, to the White Queen's sleigh, to the kids walking into the wardrobe and particularly about Aslan! Boy, the questions he asked. I slipped out when he was calming down slightly and eating his smarties.

As I walked out of the stall seating area into the foyer, I sought out a man who clearly worked in the theatre. I explained about my son's name and his love of the show, and asked if it was possible that, after the show, my son might meet the character of Aslan when he was still in costume. He said he would ask, and although he couldn't guarantee it, he took details of where we were sitting. I left it there and went back to my seat.

Once the curtains opened again, Aslan went back into mouth agape staring mode. It was a marvellous thing to watch as a mother. The box of smarties was unfinished and had been thrown into my lap which was difficult to believe. Aslan the lion was in the show much more now and Aslan my son was clutching my arm, and every now and again he would nip me in sheer excitement. Then the show was coming to an end and I was upset for Aslan. I wanted it to go on forever, and I was sure he did. However, things didn't finish at the end of the show.

A set of stairs were drawn up to the stage, almost in front of us, and every one of the characters, starting with Aslan and then the children and Mr Tumnus, came down the stairs. Aslan the lion came up to my Aslan and held his arm out to shake hands. My Aslan lifted his arm in response to have a great furry handshake and the character said something like 'Ah Aslan, it's good to meet you, how are you?' My little boy was speechless, he remained speechless whilst every character came towards him and shook his hand, and every one of them used his name. I was almost crying at the wonderful thing they were all doing to make my little boy's day. Aslan never said a word. People in the theatre were standing up and trying to see who the cast were visiting, maybe they thought it was someone important or a celebrity, and they were right as my son was certainly someone important that evening!

As we left the theatre, and for days afterwards, maybe even weeks on and off, Aslan would, out of the blue, ask how they knew his name, how they knew it was him. There was so much magic in the Theatre that night. He was totally, totally amazed.

Now we jump forward in time several years, probably about ten years, but keep in mind the theatre story. I'm living in Turkey now, but actually in Manchester Airport, waiting to board a Turkish Airline flight back to Turkey. I'd been back to the UK as I'd had a serious problem with my leg, which following a visit to the Turkish hospital had become worse. I was still living with the boys' father, but we had nothing, so my Mum and Dad had organised a flight for me so I could go back to the UK to get my leg sorted. It had been, and I was now heading home.

I boarded the plane, and my attention was drawn to an elderly lady who was boarding and sitting on the row in front of mine but on the other side of the aisle. She was sitting in the aisle seat and I instantly loved her. She was wearing such a wild mix of clothing, colours, textures, styles. A fur coat and a wonderful felt hat with a feather. Her makeup was heavy, and her lipstick was a very dark red, but she was pulling this weird and wonderful look off, even though I placed her in her late sixties, age-wise.

I couldn't help but watch her throughout the flight, I was on my own and people watching is fun sometimes, and as I watched her, she started knocking the free drinks back and much to my surprise she was speaking Turkish. I had assumed from her clothing that she was an eccentric English lady. This wasn't a direct flight to Antalya, we were flying to Istanbul with a two hour layover before the connecting flight to Antalya, which wasn't ideal, but thinking back it was out of season, and way back then there weren't the number of flights that there are today. Once we landed, and the inevitable scrum had subsided, I found myself behind this lady in the queue to get off the plane. Again, I was surprised, when I heard her now speaking English to the gentleman who was standing in front of her. This lady was certainly full of surprises. As we shuffled towards the door, she turned and started talking to me. Just general chat, but during the chat, she asked where I was going, and when I replied Antalya, she seemed pleased and said she was too. We could keep each other company as we waited for the next flight. Now I have to admit that I wasn't overly keen on this idea, but she did seem interesting and well, what could it hurt?

I did spend the next couple of hours with her, she told me the story of how she met her handsome and charming English man when he was visiting Turkey. Of her going to live in England for many years until the death of her husband. Her children.

Like myself she had two boys. We chatted about them and I discovered that one son and daughter-in-law lived across the road from the hospital my sons had been born in, in Doncaster. I also discovered that the lady, whose name was Hikmet, was travelling home to Alanya so she lived in the same city that I did.

She was still drinking quite heavily and was getting slightly drunk, and I warned her they might not let her board, but she said at her age she could get away with anything, and that she would be OK. We did indeed board, but not before we have exchanged phone numbers and promised to meet for coffee one day. We didn't sit together as we already had our seats assigned, and the plane was absolutely stuffed full. I'm glad we weren't really, as I had a problem with a man and his cheese, and it would have gotten out of hand if Hikmet had been sitting there as well.

I never saw her when I got off the plane, or as I left the airport. We were both being collected, so I didn't worry about her and headed home to see my boys. But about a week later, I got a phone call from her. She had received some paperwork and a letter from her English Building Society and asked if I could help her as she didn't really understand it. Her husband had previously looked after 'that side of things'. We met up in a café that she liked, I helped with her paperwork, and then we sat chatting for a while. Her youngest son was in Turkey somewhere, but she admitted he would only pop home occasionally and she didn't really know what he did.

We continued to meet on and off for years, only ever when she had something she needed help with, but I didn't mind. It was normally marketing information, and I think only once was it anything she needed to reply to, but I think she liked the company, and she loved chatting about her life in England. It was during one of these chats that we started discussing the theatre and she told me her daughter-in-law was regularly in plays and pantomime. I then told her the story about my eldest son, when he went to see the Lion the Witch and the Wardrobe, and how much magic there was that evening. Hikmet went quiet. I asked if she was OK and she laughed and told me her daughter-in-law had been both the characters of Susan Pevensie and Jadis The White Witch that night. She continued to explain that her daughter-in-law had told her the story of meeting a little boy named Aslan following a performance when they all shook his hand and spoke to him!

We couldn't believe how small the world is for this to actually happen, and several months later her son and daughter-in-law were coming out to Alanya to have a holiday with Hikmet. We all arranged to meet for dinner. So, Mum and Dad, Hikmet and her son and daughter-in-law, the boys and me all met up.

Aslan was, I have to say, very quiet. By now he was growing up, but Hikmet's daughter-in-law was lovely and said she remembered meeting Aslan following a request from the director to say Hello to him. It had stuck in her mind too as something magical, meeting the little boy who seemed so entranced. We all discussed it, but Aslan was too old for the magic by then.

I continued to meet up occasionally with Hikmet, until she just didn't call anymore. We had never been to each other's apartments; it just hadn't happened. I tried to call her after a long gap, but her phone was unobtainable so I could only think the worst. She was lovely woman. I never saw her unhappy apart from once when she arrived to one of our meetings in a seriously bad mood. When I asked her if she was OK, she explained that her youngest son had turned up a few weeks prior and had become involved with an English woman. What's wrong with that says I, it's no different to you and your husband? The answer she gave me made me smile. 'She's an old woman, nearly as old as me, so she's a dirty old woman!' I never did find out who the dirty old woman was. But I tried I really tried.

She was dead, but She's OK now!

During our early years in Alanya we lived in an apartment which was only a ten-minute walk from the beach, and I would try and take the boys as often as we could. I don't personally like the beach; I would be happy to tarmac over every beach everywhere. I much prefer to relax and swim in a nice pool. But at that time, I was happy to take the boys to the beach as they loved it, and in the evening it was free. Most of the time we would pack everything up and walk down about 6pm, and as we were arriving, most of the tourists were heading back to their hotels.

This was the best time, the beach was quieter, the heat of the sun wasn't so burning, and I could normally sit and relax with a book while the boys played. It didn't always work like that, because the boys would naturally drift along the beach with the normal currents, even though they were supposed to stay in front of me. So, after every third or fourth page, I would look up and have to search for the boys, followed by a wave and a 'come back this way' shout. But on the whole, our evening trips were normally good fun. I would sometimes pack up some drinks and food and we would make it into a picnic. Whatever we did, we always enjoyed our evenings on the beach. The boys might take a football with them, or a plastic lilo that someone somewhere had given them. But they always had fun. They both swam like fish, and the sea off Cleopatra beach was wonderful with high crashing waves at certain times, which the boys loved to battle through.

One evening in particular, we found our spot on the beach, unpacked the towels and I sat down with my book. We always sat on the damp sand as I hated the sand so much, and I didn't want to pay to sit on a sun bed. I was settled, and the boys were happy. About three metres away a small group of people started unpacking their bags, and then they all started arguing. I watched them, as it is always good to watch other people arguing. Well, in my opinion it is. There were two girls and two guys, and one of the girls was, it seemed, very unhappy at being on the beach. She had a lot of makeup on, and her hair was piled high in a scruffy style bun. She had a bikini on but was covered by a sarong.

The argument went on and on, and I was getting a little bored now. But just as I was starting to lose interest, one of the guys picked the whining girl up and carried her, kicking and screaming, towards the sea. She was really shouting, and really kicking, this wasn't dramatic, this was real fear. 'I don't want to go in', but in she went. Head over arse in, because when the guy got into the water, the waves took his legs from underneath him and he was over, and so she was. I'm not sure if he had meant to drop her in, but she was well and truly in now.

The boys had witnessed this, and they had stopped what they were doing to watch. The girl looked like a drowned rat, her sarong was sticking to her, one of her more than ample bosoms was sticking out of the bikini top, her makeup was running down her face, and her hair, rather than being in a nicely preened scruffy bun, was, well it was just scruffy. Kaan in particular was interested in this little scenario, especially as, when the guy got back onto his feet, he too looked a little rough. They both walked back to the other people they were with and they were now seriously arguing. Other people on the beach were now starting to take an interest, and Kaan had walked over to me and was asking what was happening.

I told him to watch, as he knew as much as I did. The train wreck girl was crying now and making a horrible noise. Her female friend was trying to help her get dry and was squeezing the Mediterranean out of the sarong, the other guy had passed her a dry towel and the guy who had dropped her in was looking very sheepish as he dried himself and was apologising a lot. The girl was, in my opinion a diva, an out and out diva. She was still crying and had also started to cough, oh what a noise. But she was on the beach. Yes, she'd had a shock, but she was in and out in seconds, she was fine really. He didn't mean to lose his legs and fall in. I think he was trying to lighten the mood if anything, but she was having none of it. At one point, Kaan said she was putting it on, whatever 'it' was. Kaan was a youngster, but he seemed to be able to see clearly what she was doing.

A few minutes later, there was a panic from the little group and when we looked again, the girl had slumped over on her towel and the other three were surrounding her and then one of them shouted for someone to help. There was a lifeguard shed nearer to the edge of the beach, and a guy came out and across to them. The four of them then picked up the young woman and carried her to the shed. She was too far away now for us to hear and see what was happening, especially since a large crowd had now gathered around her.

My interest was dwindling now, Aslan was still in the sea, he was with a couple of other kids, but Kaan had taken it upon himself to wander across to where the action was, and I watched him push to the front of the crowd where he was now standing watching. He stood watching for what seemed like a long time, then I saw him start to wander back.

I asked him what he'd been watching, what was happening? In a dead pan voice, as it seemed very serious to him, he said 'It's OK Mum. She was dead, but she's fine now!' And off he went back to play in the waves.

When Mum and Dad moved out to Alanya they lived just around the corner from the beach so on days when they were looking after the boys for me, they would all pack up and wander over to the beach. Mum is not a swimmer, but the boys, being the devils that they are, would sometimes encourage her into the edge of the sea, knowing full well that due to her small size she would quickly be knocked off her feet. They continued to do it and Mum continued to fall, and I mean literally fall, for it, even though whenever we were on the beach, we would always see people being knocked of their feet up and down the full length of the beach.

In the winter you would see lots of Turks wandering up and down on the beach with metal detectors, retrieving all the gold which was lost by the people being thrown off their feet during the summer!

Ever been to The Muhtar?

When you read this, bear in mind that I'm now of an age where, if I was a tin toy, that I would be considered to be of good vintage (not antique yet!). Maybe only the older people who have lived in, or are living in Turkey now, may recognise what I am about to talk about. But maybe this part of Turkish bureaucracy has remained, maybe it even continues to this day? I'd be interested to know.

I have to admit that amongst my favourite experiences in Alanya were rare visits to the Muhtar. When I lived there, my Muhtar was situated near the Friday market, in a tiny, tiny office. This Muhtar was responsible for the area of Saray Mahallesi. So, for anyone who lived in that area, and it was a big area, that was your Muhtar.

First, I'll try and explain what a Muhtar is. The Muhtar was like a registrar. It keeps track of where people live, along with countless other things such as births, marriages, deaths, as well as people moving about. There were always lots of reasons to visit the Muhtar. I probably haven't done them justice, but the one I had to visit was very funny in my eyes!

The entire little office revolved around a pencil that had been sharpened until only three cm remained. There was a filing system that would see Scrooge proud, and of course, there was an abundance of time and patience. Oh, and there were scissors, a Pritt stick which seemed to stand out as being very modern, and most importantly, THE STAMP, which I'll tell you about shortly.

So, now I'll set the scene. My Muhtar was located down a little alleyway, behind a stationary shop and next to a shoe shop. The doorway always littered with boxes, and stock, and old chairs with three legs and no seat part. The doorway was also invariably blocked with people, and when you finally get inside, you can understand why. The office itself was not much bigger than a small bathroom. It had two large desks in it, a shelf that clearly has not been seen under the layer of dust for at a guess, about fifty years. It had a stack of plastic chairs that were doubling up as a filing system. This always amazed me. This is the place that helps keep track of the movement of thousands of Turks and foreigners, and our paperwork is filed between plastic chairs. Maybe the fourth and fifth chairs are G- K?

Anyhow, that's the room. Inside, sitting behind the large old desks are two small old gentlemen. They should have, at their ages, been sitting on their respective balconies at home, reading the newspaper and drinking tea. However, these guys are the key workers, the staff, the Muhtar!

Now, I'm a patient sort of lady. But when you enter this particular twilight zone, you really, really have to forget about time itself. You are back to the age of pencils and paper. Imagine Scrooge and Bob Cratchett and you're almost there. Computers just don't seem to have been heard of in this office. You are back at least fifty years. Back to the time when the shelf was first put up there and the dust hadn't settled. There is no speed, no dash or no hurry in there, so be prepared.

They always needed small passport photos for everything in this office. One of these small, old gentlemen seems to have been designated as the Photo Cutter-upperer! In spite of his small stature, he had the biggest hands of any living person. But he could swiftly cut your nice photo down to a fraction of its size so that it would show off your double chin, or the bags under your eyes, really well. It was clearly a very special skill he had. Then he would staple your photo onto a piece of paper of some description, This was clearly important in the scheme of things, and he always, and I mean always, managed to get the staple straight through your eye. So, he always managed to show off your worst bits and then position the staple through your eye!

On one visit however, I remember the staple machine jammed and this became an extremely traumatic time for him. With his big hands, it clearly wasn't easy for him to sort out the problem with this small machine and the tiny staples, the tiny staples that were jamming the works up and keeping everything from moving forward. It took an age for the staple to be extracted, and for the little machine to become useful again.

The other gentleman that worked in the office seemed to be more senior. He certainly did seem to have more say, but crucially, he had THE STAMP. The stamp is a small round thing that looked like a large button. Stamps, in those days were so important. Nothing was done anywhere, Muhtar, Police Station, Tax Office, Tapu office or any other official place, without a lot of stamping. This man kept the stamp in the palm of his hand. When given a piece of paper that needed stamping, he never put the paper onto the desk and stamped it. No, no, no. Well, for one thing, the desk is so full of paperwork and books that there is no room. He seemed to prefer the process of holding the paper in the palm of one hand and kind of grinding the paper with the other hand until, on occasion, he produced a small hole and the complete paper had to be made up again!

But, after all I've said I liked these guys. I loved their little office which seemed to be in a time warp. I hope that there is always a supply of these old gentlemen to step in and take over from the Muhtars as they leave, die or retire. We should all be able to experience a trip to the Muhtars office!

I'm Sorry, Was I Speeding?

Twice during my life in Turkey, I was pulled over for speeding. Me! Speeding? How dare they? But they did dare!

The first time, I was in a bright red Ford Fiesta. I did stick out like a sore thumb, as most of the cars on the road with me back then were old bangers. I am talking about the years before the real property and tourist boom. The boom that changed everything, when lots of new and expensive cars appeared almost overnight.

I was on my way home from Belek. I had started work the previous day when I had driven to Belek. I had done an overnight airport transfer with departures followed by another transfer for arrivals. I had managed about two hours sleep and a shower. I had then done a welcome meeting in two different hotels about five miles apart. Now I was on my two-hour drive home.

I was almost back in Alanya, driving along the spectacular coast road, when I was flagged over. Bugger, bugger and double bugger. I just wanted to go home. I was tired and had been wearing my Rep's uniform for way too long now. It wasn't the best design; I think it must have been a man who designed it. It was made from thick polyester that stuck to you as soon as you walked outside. The skirt was knee length, with a lovely thick lining so every time you stood up you had to pull your skirt down because it was stuck to your arse. Lovely in Alanya! Anyway, I've gone off subject yet again!

I pulled over, along side another car, onto a piece of land just off the side of the road. There were two policemen. Unfortunately, no one that I knew or recognised. Pfff was the sound I made. Now, how should I handle this? Did I get out or just open the window? The woman in the other car next to me had stepped out, so I thought maybe I'd better to the same. I stepped out of the car. Then suddenly it hit me. I was in my rep's uniform, so I put a plan into action. 'I'm sorry, have I done something wrong?' I asked in my wonderful Yorkshire accent. One of the policemen stepped towards me and spoke in Turkish. 'Can you speak Turkish? You've been caught speeding; do you have your driving licence and passport?' Of course, I could speak enough Turkish then to understand him, but instead I said 'sorry', I don't understand'. 'Have I done anything wrong?'

The policeman, being in his uniform, looked as hot and bothered as I felt. I don't think he was having a particularly good day. He turned to the other policeman and the conversation went something like 'Bloody reps, they come here and work and earn more than us and don't even bother to learn the language. She doesn't understand me, what do I do?' The other policeman, who was dealing with the lady from the other car, shrugged and said, 'I don't know.'

The lady from the other car then broke into the conversation. She said I should be given a ticket the same as she was, regardless whether I was foreign or not. I, at the same time, stood asking 'Was I speeding, have I done something wrong?' I said it quite a lot, as all I could see was the commission I'd made earlier that day selling trips of various descriptions going up in thin air if I had to pay a fine. The policeman came back towards me. Doing a pantomime type thing, he said 'Driving Licence, Passport' a couple of times. The lady in the car next to me was having her ticket written out. She was adamant that if she was getting a ticket, then so should I. To be fair, I should have, but there's nothing fair about speeding tickets. Anyway, I was doing my best 'just got off the plane, don't speak a word of Turkish' show.

The policeman then gave up and said 'Oh, please, just go. Go!' I almost jumped in my car and drove off, but then stopped myself and said one more my little line. 'I'm sorry, was I speeding?' The reply, with an arm wave was 'go!' I stood blankly looking at him until he walked towards me, opened my car door and practically threw me inside. Once more, he did a wide wave of his arm to motion me to go. So, who am I to argue? I went! As I pulled away, I could still see the woman arguing with them and had a pretty good idea what she was saying!

My commission was safe, but I never speeded along that road again. I certainly would never have gotten away with that twice!

There was another occasion, however, when I was caught speeding. But in my defence, I was driving down a very steep hill. You don't think that's a defence, eh? OK, well I'll explain. The boys and I were on one of our Jollies. This time I had taken them East and we were staying in a hotel in Iskenderun for a night, then we'd be going on to Osmaniye for two nights. I wanted to take them to Hatay to see the scenes I'd been lucky enough to experience, one of them being St Peters Church which is sometimes called the first Church ever. We got to Hatay, and I showed them the church. All I got was an astounding 'it's OK' when I asked them what they thought. We did have more success in the bazaar, which was a fraction of the prices we were paying in Alanya. We'd had something to eat and then we'd set off back to Osmaniye, and our hotel. It hadn't been the educational super holiday I imagined, and I did think that next time we would be off back to Marmaris or Kusadasi.

We were in a small, rented saloon car. Both boys were in the back because they had argued, as always, as to who would be in the front. So, neither of them were. I realty don't know where we were, other than somewhere between Hatay and Osmaniye, but it was a very long, very steep hill, and the road was a dual carriageway. I was about halfway down. I didn't think I was going particularly fast, but I clearly was as there were two policemen standing in front of me and they indicated that I should pull over. One was in uniform and the other in normal clothing. There were no other cars. Bugger! I quickly turned to the boys, told them to open their windows and start talking English, they had been sitting arguing in Turkish for most of the journey so far. They looked at me and asked why, but when I said something like 'just do it guys', they clearly picked up on the fact that I was serious.

Now imagine this. The boys, who are half Turkish anyway, had been living in Turkey for several years now. They were black from always being outside all summer. They had the looks of their Dad, the same colour, and they were wearing Turkish clothing. You know, the clothing that was for sale to tourists everywhere in Turkey. They didn't look anything like foreigners, they looked like pure Turks. But when they spoke in English, it was pure Yorkshire! So here goes, similar thing to the first time I'd been stopped, but this time I remained in the car and opened the window. Once more I got the 'have you got your passport and driving licence, where are you staying?' Again, I burst into my 'Have I done something wrong?' routine. This went on for a few minutes, and during this one of the boys offered to help me translate! Nooo! I say calmly, you just carry on chatting guys!

The policeman who was in uniform and who was trying to deal with me gave up and wandered off to speak with the man not in uniform, who I presumed was his boss. They exchanged a few words. I was guessing it was something similar to the conversation a few years previously in Alanya, when I'd been stopped while I was repping! The man in plain clothes came over to the car this time. He popped his head down and looked in. He then walked to the back of the car and popped his head down again. Bless them, my boys were in great form. They were having a real argument, but this time it was in Yorkshirese. Perfect! He walked back to the front of the car and said something to me in German. I was so wanting to laugh but didn't. I changed my line to 'I'm sorry I don't understand you'. This went on a few minutes until he stood up, and tapping the top of my car, he motioned me to leave. I did!

I started laughing once we were out of sight and near the bottom of the hill. The boys, as young as they were, had by then understood what I'd done. They said I was bad! Nooo I wasn't, I was just tight. We laughed most of the way back as they took it in turns and mimicked me saying 'I'm sorry was I speeding?'

Rain in Kemer

When I was working for Airtours, back in the day, I was doing OK financially. Well, I was paying my rent and my bills, and the boys and I were eating, so that was good. But I was always looking for more ways to increase the money I could make. I had changed from doing transfers for Airtours, to being a part-time rep for the resort of Belek. Belek was a great resort, miles of five-star hotels, all beach fronts, but behind miles of forest. Lots of golf courses had been built and were still being established when I was repping there. As with most holiday companies, I guess, the excursions aren't actually run by Airtours. They have a Turkish business partner who organises the excursions, employs the buses and coaches, and the guides to go with the holidaymakers. As Belek was only a small resort, there weren't huge numbers of holidaymakers arriving each week, so I made a deal with Murat, the guy who ran the excursions.

Murat and I agreed that, if I sold any of the trips at my weekly welcome meetings, I would then guide them. This meant that I was paid for each excursion I guided, unless it was a trip to Pammukale because that needed a profession guide. Some of the trips I was selling at the welcome meetings included a boat trip from Manavgat, which didn't need a guide, and a trip to the Duden Waterfall which included the spice market in Antalya, which I could guide. There also was a coach trip to Side and a boat trip to Kemer, both of which I could guide. The only problem with the boat trip to Kemer was that it was on a Saturday, and I really didn't want to spend any more time away from the boys if I could help it. Murat and I agreed that I would guide it without payment, but that the boys could come on the trip too. The boys and I were able to spend a fun day together, and meals and drinks would be paid for, so I was happy with that arrangement. The boys loved being on boats, so they were happy. It was a long day, though. We were two hours away from the hotels in Belek, and after we'd picked up the holidaymakers coming with us, it was another two hours to Kemer. Then the same in reverse at the end of the day, so we had a 6am start and would normally not get home much before 8pm, when the boys would shower and disappear off to bed as they were absolutely worn out.

I have talked about the Duden and Side trips in other stories, but I loved all of these trips. I never felt like I was working as I loved being with the holidaymakers and passing on all the knowledge I had about Turkey and that part of the world. I knew I was doing something right, as many of these wonderful people re-booked to do the same trips for their second week. I got to know some of them really well. I was lucky, although I was broke and on my own with the boys, life at that time felt good.

One particular Saturday trip to Kemer sticks in my mind for a few reasons. The boys and I were up and showered early, and we walked across to the Travel Agent office where the buses waited for their guides. We could almost see the office from our balcony, but we could easily see the buses queuing up on the road outside. That week, I had sold lots of seats, so we had an Isuzu bus which were easier to guide from. On other weeks, we had a Sprinter minibus, which were harder to work from. But if I was on full form, we would sometimes get a grown-up bus, a big forty-five seater coach. It was normally the same driver on the minibus, a nice guy called Mehmet. On the Izuzu buses, which seated about 28 people, it would be one or other of my two of my favourite drivers, Kismet and Ahmet. They were good friends of mine, and the big coaches would either be a Dervish, which a great name for a bus, or a Mustafa. All of these drivers were really nice guys. Like most of the drivers then, I don't know if it's any different now, they came to the resorts to work for a company during the summer season. They lived on their tips most of the time, they were given meals from some of the hotels and restaurants they took the guests into, and a lot of them slept in the baggage holds of their buses. This meant that they could send home every penny they possibly could. I always explained this to holidaymakers and tried my best to encourage them to leave a tip. The drivers sometimes hurt themselves lugging heavy cases out of the holds, and there was no sick pay, they just had to carry on. They spent months away from wives, girlfriends, kids and families, and sometimes holidaymakers just climb on the bus and don't even acknowledge the driver. They leave rubbish all over the place, occasionally spill drinks and occasionally vomit. All of which, the driver has to clean up. Not the best job ever, but they remained happy and friendly.

This particular morning, the boys were happy because they saw Kismet standing near his bus drinking water. They liked him, he was as dry as a bone with his sense of humour, and he liked the boys too. Good mornings were passed, and we set off to the hotels. We probably had a couple of hotels to collect from, I looked after three of the hotels on that stretch, but they were spread out over a few miles. Once everyone was on board, the boys were introduced. I always explained why they were with us, no one ever minded, and the boys became something of a novelty themselves. During the day everyone would ask them what they thought of living in Alanya, what school was like, how they coped with the language and many, many more random questions. They were always happy to chat with people, and they made me proud how they dealt with the mainly unwanted attention. They hadn't reached the age where girls were on their radars yet, which I was always pleased about!

When we arrived in Kemer, which is a lovely resort, the driver would drop us off at the edge of the harbour area and we would all wander down to the boat like a crocodile made up of school kids. Well, that's what it always reminded me of. The bus drivers were, if they chose to, allowed on the boat as well, as there was nothing else planned for them due to the location. We were all on board and the kids were very happy to see Kismet running down to the boat to join us. He did that often but would normally just find a comfortable shady area to sit, watch and nap the day away.

I, on the other hand, had work to do. I would explain to everyone on board where the toilets were, what the rules with the drinks were (it was an all-inclusive day), what the etiquette was at lunch time, what the plan for the trip was, where we would head, and what we would be doing. There were sometimes guests from some of the hotels in Kemer on board too. A friend of mine was the rep in Kemer, and she would join us if she had any free time which unfortunately wasn't often. I would also tell the guests the names of the crew. By this time, we were normally out of the harbour, so it was sit back and enjoy the scenery, unless anyone had a problem. Our first stop would be for swimming.

On each trip, smaller boats pulled up alongside us whenever we stopped for breaks. One sold fresh fruit, cut beautifully and proffered on paper plates. Another would sell ice cream, and have a small freezer run by a tiny generator on board. They must have needed to replenish a hundred times a day. On board our boat there was always one of the staff taking photos. To younger people this may sound strange, but this was back in the day when there were very few mobile phones about, and none of them had cameras. Yes, those days! The photographer would take pics of everyone on the boat, whether they wanted it taking or not. At the first swimming stop, the photographer would put all the films into a watertight bag along with his clothes, and he would dive off, swim to the shore and vanish to get the photos developed. He would normally reappear at the next stop and then spend the rest of the trip wandering around, showing people their photos and selling them.

There was also a man who turned up to sell our guests a ride on his Jet-Ski. Chatting with this guy, I discovered his name was Ertan. He found out that I loved Jet-Ski's, but that I had only used them when I had visited Turkey as a tourist, never since I had moved there. He and I made a deal too. I know, deals galore, but that was my life back then! If I encouraged or helped him sell rides, then I could have a go for free. Cool!

The first time the boys and I did this was about the third trip into the summer, as it took me that long to get to talk to him and make our deal. I'll tell you about this shortly. Make a tea and we will get going.

Back to the particular boat trip. We arrived at the swimming place and anchors were dropped, people stripped off shorts, sarongs, glasses etc and whoosh we were all in the water, including the boys and I as it was getting hot. We were all having a great time. One of the crew had thrown a ball in and we were playing with that. Then something happened which was really odd. It started raining. This was wrong on so many levels, not only was it interfering with out fun, but it was unknown for it to rain in the summer. I lived in Turkey for ten years and can't remember another day of rain in the summer!

Everyone climbed back onto the boat and wrapped themselves up, as it was cold. The sky was overcast, we had just stepped out of the sea, and even wrapped in towels it was cold. Aslan and Kaan had chattering teeth even. It was like this for a fair length of time and people were starting to drink, not water, or tea that the crew had just made, but beer and the local spirits that were included for the day. I could see the crew getting anxious, and when I asked what the problem was, they explained that they were worried about the drinks running out, for two reasons, one that people would get mad and bad mouth the trip to the operators, and the second that they probably wouldn't make any money from the trip if they had to totally re-stock all the drinks. I felt bad. what could I do?

I joined the boys who had gone to talk to Kismet. He was still fully dressed and was laughing at all the cold people. It was then I got the idea. I asked the boys to trust me, put their towels down and follow me, which they did. I walked to the side of the boat, in the pouring rain and I jumped in. No elegant dive, just a fat bird holding her nose, heading in. Being heavy I always sank a long way, and I always wondered if I'd ever get back to the surface. But I did, and I looked up and encouraged the boys to follow me. They did, but they did those super-dooper dives that they had perfected. It was still raining but it was warmer in the sea than it was standing with a towel around our shoulders. The guests on the boat got the idea, and before long most of the people who had been in the water when it started raining were back in there. We carried on the ball game and didn't even notice when the rain stopped. We had great fun that day. When I did climb back on the boat, the crew said they were really thankful, and that the boys and I had saved the day.

I told you earlier about Ertan and the Jet-Ski. Well, the boys had never been on a Jet-Ski as when we came as tourists, they weren't big enough, and I had never been able to afford such a luxury since we had lived there. This was our chance. It was the third Kemer boat trip, and a few of the guests had been for rides, and Ertan shouted me over. I asked if I could take the kids with me. 'Of course,' was his reply. They were both up for it, and we all climbed onboard the Jet-Ski. I did this from the side of the boat, but I was always frightened that I would fall off in the middle of nowhere, miles away from the boat and not be able to drag my fat ass back onto the Jet-Ski. Fortunately, I never did, so I was never able to find out!

Aslan climbed on and we decided that Kaan, being the youngest, should go in the middle. I turned the throttle and off we went. I tried not to go too fast with the boys being there, but I do love speed! We moved away from the boat, and imagine, nothing, absolutely nothing, in our way. No other boats, no coastline, not even any sign of a big wave. Bliss, and perfect for a Jet-Ski. I turned the throttle some more, and we sped up, I could hear Aslan shouting 'faster Mum, go faster' and he was whooping and totally enjoying himself. But a few minutes later I could hear Kaan shouting and trying to make himself heard above Aslan's whooping. 'Slow down Mum we're going to crash! We're going to crash!' Aslan was in pieces, laughing, and I have to admit it was funny. There was nothing or no one to crash into. In Kaan's defence, though, he wasn't very old. And as a grown man he now loves speed, so he did get over it.

I didn't want to give him any kind of phobia, so I turned and headed back towards the boat. But Aslan and I hadn't had enough and we seemed to be on the same wavelength. Once we got back to the boat, we both lifted Kaan off and put him in the water. That sounds better than we threw him off, anyway. We stayed a minute to make sure he was climbing back onto the boat, then I turned the throttle again and Aslan and I were off. We had a few minutes left, and we made sure we got some speed up. The funny thing is, now that Aslan is a man, he's the cautious slower one! Kids eh, go figure!

We had a great season on those trips, and as well as the free Jet-Ski rides, guests would sometimes approach and ask me whether, if they paid, would I be willing to take their kids on? Err yeah! It's a hard life, but someone's got to do it.

Camel Conspiracy

How do you feel about Camels? Love them? Hate them? Have no particular feeling about them? Well, I have mixed feelings. I do believe they were put on earth for a reason, a reason other than making large body builders look stupid…. I'll come to that shortly. But for the life of me, I can't really say anything very nice about them.

I worked for Airtours in Turkey, back in the days when we were allowed to travel and go on holidays (I am writing this during 2020). But way back then, one of the resorts I was a rep for was called Belek, which was predominately a golf resort set on the southern coast of Turkey about 40 minutes from Antalya airport. There were never a lot of arrivals due to the nature of the resort. However, I had done a deal with the owner of the company that ran the excursions, and if I sold enough excursions during my welcome meeting on a Monday morning, I could guide those trips. So I tried very hard to sell the interesting and fun excursions so that I could make money guiding during the week.

One of the excursions on my list to sell was a trip which went to the spice market in Antalya and then on to the Duden waterfall. The excursion trips were always early starts for me since I lived in Alanya, which was a two-hour drive away from the Belek resort. I would be up very early and walk across to the office where the coaches or minibuses would wait. This was followed by a two-hour drive to the hotels in Belek where I would round up the customers who were joining me on the tour for the day. Once we had collected everyone, it was an hour, sometimes slightly more, to get to the car park near the spice market in Antalya.

We would spend about ninety minutes wandering around the market together. It was a magical place. A covered market with almost every stall containing neatly piled brightly coloured piles of spices. Boxes and piles of every sort of Turkish delight you could imagine. Nuts, dates, fruit that was like sweets strung up everywhere. You could ask to try almost anything and the stall holders were happy to let you, pleased to show you things you didn't understand and happy to sell anything from a tiny amount of saffron to the biggest bag of pistachio nuts.

It was always busy, but most of the people shopping were tourists, as it really was a tourist attraction rather than a place where locals would shop to buy their everyday needs. But nevertheless, it was a great market, and the prices hadn't been overinflated, so many purchases were made. As we walked out of the market, there was a small but clean and friendly café where I would always recommend people to grab a drink while we waited for the bus to appear (I always called them when we were on our way out of the market as they parked a small distance away). We would normally sit and review our purchases for a few minutes before jumping back on the coach. Almost every week during the season I would inevitably find myself once again explaining what saffron was, and why the saffron threads were so expensive. For anyone that doesn't know, saffron is made from the flower of the crocus, each flower has three stamen: thread like things in the centre. Eighty thousand crocus flowers must be grown, cared for, hand harvested and processed to make one pound of saffron! I knew this as I had been incredibly lucky to be able to stop whilst driving past a crocus field near Safronbolu, a place in Turkey near the Black sea where the Crocus grow.

This was during one of my many travels with my then partner Cevat, driving from Ankara to Izmit. He asked if I wanted to see the flowers. Of course I did. We travelled out of our way for about fifty minutes, but it was well worth the time and effort. I was absolutely stunned. Fields and fields of beautiful light purple flowers, tiny little crocus. We climbed out of the car to have a look and there were a couple of ladies working in the field picking the flowers and dropping them into baskets. When they saw us, they were happy to walk across and show us and explain. Each flower had three dark orange/red stamen in the middle and this was where the saffron came from. I can only imagine the labour that goes into producing saffron and I have never moaned since when I'm buying saffron threads!

Anyway, with my saffron explanation finished, we all would hop back onto the bus and drive the few miles to Duden waterfall. This is a lovely waterfall which is situated in a park which is a few acres of woodlands and lovely scenery with a river running through it. The waterfall forms the start of the river. It is said that it's the waterfall where the Timotei shampoo TV advert was filmed, but I don't know if that's true because, on most days the flow of the water could knock your head off! However, it is a really nice place to visit. The buses would pull into a dead-end road opposite the gates of the waterfall park, and stop there to let everyone off. They would then drive off and park up somewhere else for a couple of hours before returning to collect everyone, so it worked well.

As everyone climbed off the bus, I would go ahead along the road, past the camels and across the road to buy the tickets to get into the park. Then I would go back past the camels and wait for the customers. Now we will revisit the camels in a second, but I'd like to explain that once in the park, we would walk through the woodlands, and down to the waterfall. It was possible to walk along the back of the falls through a tunnel, and then back again, and on a hot day it was a really pleasant thing to do. We would then walk along the river's edge, over a bridge and back again along the riverside, climbing gently up the hillside to the top and back out. A wonderful place to visit, especially in the heat as being under trees and near a river was a nice way to get out of the sun and the heat for a short while.

Once we were out of the park and back across the road, we came to the place where my arch enemies the camels were hanging out. A group of young lads would stand on the pavement at the dead end of the road, and they had a group of four. maybe five camel. A different number every week, but always there.

Now, these camels all hated me. I don't know why. I never did find out, and the guys who were with them were always amused and they tried, and I tried, everything. The first few times I walked past them, they flapped their horrid lips, spitting and making noises and I thought it was just a fluke. The guys pulled them back and stopped them, but they continued to do that every time I walked past, and I mean every time.

Over the two seasons I did this tour it actually got worse. That proved to be difficult, as many of the guests I was with wanted to stop. The guys were there to make money, they would let you stand next to, or sit on a camel for a small amount of money. Visitors could also sit on one and have a walk down to the end of the road and back if they paid a little more money.

I needed to stay with my guests, but the bloody camels didn't want me to. Even if they were sitting nicely, as soon as I arrived they would try and get up, they would spit, they would make the most obscene noises and they would, if they got near enough try and bite me. They had farted on me several times as well. The guys advised lots of solutions, I even fed them food that the guys gave. Well, I tried to feed them, but after one of them nearly took my fingers off, I threw the rest of the food at them! I tried changing my footwear, and I know that sounds mad, but the guys said maybe they didn't like my clip clopping noise of my rep style court shoes. I think they were taking the micky, but I did it anyway. I changed my perfume, I changed the direction I approached them from so I wouldn't sneak up on them from behind. I even whispered when I was near them, maybe they didn't like my Yorkshire accent. I was almost ready to change my bloody name, but nothing worked!

The guys had said that if my guests used the camels enough, as a treat I could have a 'free' ride at the end of the season. Ha, yeah that would be great. They laughed when I told them I would rather poke my eye out with a blunt spoon, but maybe that was the way I said that half in English and half in Turkish.

My guests would, every week, walk across the road towards the buses after their walk around the park, but on the way they would 'oh' and 'ah' at the camels, and lots would stand next to them, hug them and 'kiss' them (which was really those smelly-breathed nit-infested animals from hell licking my guests).

Ewwww! But my guests were generally enjoying having their photos taken with them. The more adventurous would even want to climb onboard the evil, spiteful, ship-of-the-desert devils. These were interesting times, especially when the 'adventurous' guest was a body builder type with little or no neck. These guys always wanted to have a go. They almost always fell off with no elegance at all, making the loudest noises. I clearly remember one guy who was seriously into his gym visits. But there are no camels in gyms, he was out of his depth and he had clearly been taken by surprise. He struggled to hold on and stay on when the pig from hell unfolded its long scabby legs and rose up, throwing the gym guy forward. He expelled a very girly squeal which made everyone laugh. He then overcompensated by leaning back which made him bob about like one of those figurines with its head on a spring. Now everyone was watching him, and everyone was laughing.

In his defence though, he was still hanging on when the devil hound started walking, urged on by one of the young minders with a stick. I have to say, in my opinion the stick wasn't nearly big enough or heavy enough. Just saying! The gym guy swayed about in that odd way that people riding these deadly critters do, but he was smiling and looking confident as they turned around and started heading back.

Meanwhile I was having my own battle, with one of the fat twatting things sitting there spitting and muttering at me! I moved out of range and it looked like it was planning to get up and follow me until the guy beside it, using his stick, made the damned thing reconsider its choices. It slumped back down, still giving me verbal abuse and farting loudly.

The gym guy was almost back, and his wife was laughing and taking photos, shouting up to him to look this way and wave, and smile, and well, lots of instructions. But I never heard the one that should have been issued, which was to hang on for dear life. Although I had witnessed what followed hundreds of times, this was one of the best. There was always a gap left for the returning death-trap to park in, or whatever it is that camels do when they fold up and sit down. The returning spit-machine walked towards it's parking space, and as usual its rider was totally unprepared for the next move. He just wasn't in sync, and as the camel folded it's front scabby knees underneath itself and lurched forward, the guy did some really classic gymnastic moves, and although I doubt these moves have names they would probably have gained him 9.9 points in the Olympic Games. But his final dismount from the beast let him down badly.

His move was a double somersault, followed by a back flip, with some weird twist involving arm waving accompanied by such a super dooper squeal. He then hit the pavement with such a thud that the thought did flash into my mind that I hadn't yet paid a visit to Antalya hospital. But credit where credit is due, he jumped up brushing his clothes down and laughing, but I'm sure he must have hurt himself as he fell from a height and went down very heavy. He did have a graze on his knee and claimed that was his only injury though.

This wasn't the end of his humiliation though. His wife set off telling him how stupid he was getting on the stupid f*****g thing in the first place. She gave him a hard time most of the way back to the hotel, but the other guests thought he'd been an absolute superstar.

My last dealings with the long-legged toady creatures was a few weeks before the end of one of the summer seasons. This particular week the guys had a trainee scabby-leg with them. It was a baby but was still a pretty big thing. I didn't know at first, but as I dashed past the group of them on this particular day on my way to buy the park tickets, the trainee got up. It wasn't on a leash or fastened down because they normally just follow their Mums about. As I dashed across the road to the park, the trainee started to run after me. Now, it could be said that it was just following me, but I will stay adamant that it was chasing me, because of what happened when I reached the other side of the road. The man selling tickets in his little glass kiosk looked scared to death. He opened his door and ushered me in before I was run over by the marauding baby. That was a close call, and needless to say, I didn't take up the very kind offer of a free ride a few weeks later when the season finished. I'm from Yorkshire, we do like free things, but even I draw the line.

A Gentle Lady?

During my life in Turkey I was lucky to make lots of friends, one of these ladies was a gentle lady by the name of Shirley, her partner was a Turk by the name of Yusuf. Sadly, neither of them are with us now, Shirley passed first, and not long after Yusuf passed. I met Shirley when she and Yusuf had opened a small café/restaurant close to where my tour business was located. We got to know each other and tried to help each other out. Their café was located next door to a large hotel which took Airtours guests. My shop was at the bottom of a road where there was another hotel taking Airtours guests. Between us, Shirley and I we were talking to lots of Brits, even though the year in question was a quiet one due to wars and terrorism. Shirley would tell her guests about me and my shop, and the people I spoke to regarding tours would be directed round to Shirley's café.

I often sat chatting with Shirley. She was such a gentle soul but had lots of stories to tell. She was just a nice lady. The word nice just doesn't do it, but that's what she was.

Towards the end of the season, during one of our chats, Shirley asked if I wanted to join her and Yusuf on a night out. Yusuf was a quiet man, but he was also a big giant of a man, rather scary looking. He and Shirley were a happy couple, and I liked them both so I agreed, especially when they said they were going to one of my favourite places where there was a live singer I really liked. It was a Turkish nightclub, and it was very rare that you would see tourists in there. Dark, smoky, and raki was the drink of choice.

On the evening we were going out together, we'd planned that I'd meet Shirley and Yousef at the nightclub. The evenings didn't start until at least 11pm, sometimes later. I struggle to believe I was able to do that, to stay up until the early hours of the morning and then most times go to work early the next day. Nowadays, if I'm up past 10pm I always expect the 'late night' monitor to be knocking on the door to see what I'm up to, or to be asleep in front of some TV programme we are watching. Life is different when we are away on holidays, but again it's normally early nights as we cram so much into each day. But back then, well I was made of stronger stuff, clearly!

We sat in the nightclub; Yusuf was drinking raki. I'm not 100% sure what Shirley was drinking, but she liked a drink just as much as the rest of us. I was, I guess, drinking my normal tipple which was Turkish Vodka and cola. The night was pleasant, good company and great music, until Shirley and I noticed a bit of commotion behind Yusuf's chair. People on the next table were pushing and shoving everyone around them so they could try and squeeze two further chairs around their table. That didn't work in this nightclub, as it was already so tightly packed, and each table had four chairs. We were on the side of a little space which was sometimes a dance floor and this table of thug-like people were between us and a large window which looked out onto Alanya harbour. There was just nowhere to fit in extra people.

Yusuf turned and said something to them especially when he saw that the commotion was due to two 'ladies of the night' trying to gain a seat at someone else's cost. These ladies were predominantly eastern European or Russians back then. They tended only to be seen really late at night. Normally, they didn't hurt anyone and kept to themselves, but this evening they were annoying both us and two other tables on each side of them, which were also full. No one could move anywhere! Then, and it all seemed to happen so quickly in front of us, one guy at the offending table slugged Yusuf about the head!

I was shocked, but this was Turkey. Turkey is a hard place to live, many arguments are decided with a physical altercation. And particularly in these sorts of places. Their table erupted, our table was overturned onto the dancefloor and several other people now seemed to have become involved. Poor Yusuf seemed to have three men on him and one of the 'ladies of the night' was shouting at Shirley. The whole place had quickly become similar to an old cowboy film where everyone just fights for the sake of it, without really knowing what triggered it off. I decided it was probably better to go outside, the door led straight onto the pavement, and I thought it might be beneficial to get out of this chaos. But just as I was leaving I saw Yusuf swing a heavy ashtray above his head and it make contact with one of the antagonists from the other table.

I dragged Shirley outside, we stayed a while waiting for Yusuf to come out, or for the cowboy saloon to calm down. But he didn't come out, and it never calmed down, so I asked Shirley if she was OK and I left for home.

I saw Shirley and Yusuf a couple of days later, and both were laughing about the whole thing. Apparently, there had been some serious name calling before they clocked Yusuf on the head. It all calmed down eventually, but only after quite a while. Shirley said that they all sat back down and enjoyed the rest of the night, once tables and chairs had been picked back up and the floor swept.

A couple of months later, Shirley asked again if I wanted to go out with them. This time it was for New Year's Eve. My usual partner in crime, Jules, who I normally would have been going out with, was back in the UK for Christmas and the New Year, so this year I had found myself alone for the holidays. I don't think I really minded the thought of not going out very much. I had had a spectacular year. Besides, I was a little worried about going out with them again, after the Cowboy Saloon incident. I told Shirley this, and she said it definitely wouldn't happen again because Yusef's brother, who was a policeman in Hatay where Yusuf came from, would be there. I'd met his brother briefly earlier that year. He was a nice guy too, so I said OK and we planned our night out.

New Year's Eve arrived, and Shirley, Yusuf and Yusuf's brother, whose name I can't remember for the life of me, picked me up in his car. Off we went to a Casino. Now, anyone who knows Turkey will know that Casinos are illegal, and they had been turned into large nightclubs when I lived out there, but for some reason they still kept the name Casino.

This was a nice place, out of Alanya, just off the main coastal road on the way to Mahmutlar. I'd never been before, and we took our seats and were quickly having a good time. There was live music and a good atmosphere. During the evening though, there was a man who would come talk to Yusuf and his brother, then he would wander off again. He was sitting at a different table. I really didn't make too much of it until we asked for our bill at the end of the night. When it arrived, I'd already arranged to pay my way and they started adding up what we had eaten and drank. I asked what was wrong as there seemed to be some confusion. The guys got up and walked over to the other man's table, leaving Shirley and I not really knowing what had happened.

Several minutes later, Yusuf, his brother, the man who had been coming to our table and a chef with a bloody enormous doner kebab knife, all came bursting through one of the doors! What the hell? Not again? Now I can't stress enough that this isn't the normal way nights out go, I must have just been lucky!

Guests were already leaving, so many of them just stepped it up a gear and left more quickly. But staff now seemed to be getting involved in this fracas. Shirley and I still had no idea what was happening and I suggested we should go outside. That evening, and this is important, Yusuf was wearing jeans, a white shirt and a tan coloured leather waistcoat. I was in front of Shirley and left the building and walked along the path and sat on a wall. Shirley came out behind me, sat for a few minutes then decided that she needed the loo and went back to the door, but they wouldn't let her back in. She wandered off round the back of the building and had a wee in their garden.

As I sat on the wall, the scene unfolded in front of me. The characters appeared one by one; it was like a bad Turkish movie this time. The man in chef's whites was running around with a doner kebab knife and Yusuf's brother was running into the street shouting, 'I'm a policeman'. People were coming out onto their balconies opposite the club. Some even pulled chairs up, ready to watch this show. I was sitting in prime position to watch. Yusuf appeared and his waistcoat had been ripped right up the back, from the hem at the bottom to the neckline, but it was still hanging in there, flapping about! Other men, including the man who had constantly appeared at our table, were now outside, together with several of the staff who had earlier been nice, polite waiters. They were all throwing punches at each other, some were landing, most were like the fight scene between Colin Firth and Hugh Grant in the Bridget Jones movie!

As I watched, I noticed that Yusuf had now lost part of his shirt and was wearing half a shirt with a weird flappy looking waistcoat over it. Shirley was sitting swinging her legs and didn't seem at all bothered. I wondered if my little gentle friend had witnessed scenes like this many times before. Then a police car pulled up! Pffff could it get any worse? Actually, it got slightly better. A policeman got out of the car and it was Mehmet, a guy who was big friends with my friend Jules, and I knew him quite well. He saw me, and as the other policeman in the car headed into the chaos, Mehmet joined me on the wall. In his very best English, he asked 'what are you doing Tina?' I really wasn't sure how to answer.

Another police car appeared. Yusuf's brother was still defending himself from the doner kebab knife, using part of a shrub he'd grabbed and still shouting 'I'm a policeman'. I don't think the chef with the knife really meant business, though. Yusuf was now completely bare from the waist up. Strangely, the man who seemed to have caused most of this for whatever reason, the man who kept visiting our table, was sitting in the passenger seat of Yusuf's brother's car! The surrounding balconies were now full of spectators. I challenge anyone to explain that!

The three policemen eventually managed to calm everyone down. The kebab knife and the bush seemed to be in police custody, and Shirley had wandered into the street and found Yusuf's waistcoat, or what was left of it. I asked what she would do with it, and she answered saying she'd have it repaired. Knowing what can be done in Turkey, she probably did. One of the police cars left when the movie had finished, sorry, I mean when the fight had finished. Yusuf and his brother were standing talking to the odd chap who was still sitting in their car. Shirley joined them, and said we were heading home, so I should get in. I laughed, yeah right! Instead, Mehmet said he'd drop me off on the way back to the police station.

Yusuf, his brother, the odd man and Shirley set off. Mehmet and the other policeman kindly took me home. I did get a bit annoyed though, when he put his blue lights on when he stopped to let me out outside my apartment block, but he said it was just so everyone in the building saw me coming home in a police car!

When I got to the bottom of the story, it seemed that the odd man who kept visiting our table had been putting all his food and drinks on our bill. He was the brother of the chef with the knife. Once he'd been caught out, it seemed everyone got involved. Had we not been adding up the bill to split it, maybe he would have got away with it. Funny thing was, we never paid out bill!

My friend Jules came home a few days later. She asked me what I'd one for New Year's Eve. 'Errr, let's get a coffee Jules, and I'll tell you all about it'.

I loved Shirley, the gentle lady, and I was so sorry when I heard she had passed away, but I never went out with them again.

When Making Breakfast Isn't As Easy As Opening A Box!

When I first moved to live in Turkey it was November 1998. It feels like a lifetime ago sometimes. I had a three-year-old and a six year old with me. And I was about to start a hard chapter of my life. Hard in lots of ways and I'm sure it's so much different now, but still, for people moving to any foreign country, it's not a thing to take lightly.

Food was one of the most challenging things back then. Having two small children, they needed familiar things. Although they had been introduced to Turkish food during holidays as well as back in the UK, they were small boys. Trying to explain to them why they couldn't have fishfingers or beefburgers was not an easy thing.

I'd been taught by my then mother-in-law, how to make a few dishes. I could make good kofte, which I tried to use as a substitute for beefburgers sometimes. I could make Manti, which is a Turkish type of ravioli. I could make that really well. My husband loved it, and I had made it a lot in the UK before we moved out to Alanya. Once, whilst on holiday in Izmir, I made Manti, and my mother-in-law was so astounded that she filled a plate up and took it up and down the street showing people! The only problem with Manti is that the boys and myself didn't like it, so that was not on the top of my menu for us.

We found Migros, which, way back then, was the only vaguely European style of supermarket. That was it. There were a lot of local Turkish style shops, but of course there was nothing very familiar in them! So, the challenge was on. Cheese was a lifesaver as, like me, the boys loved cheese back then. It took me a long time to discover why all the cheeses were such wildly different prices, and what was what. For those of you who don't know or have never really thought about it when shopping to self-cater, the cost depends mostly on the milk used. If the cheese is really cheap, it's probably made using skimmed milk. The next most expensive cheese is made with semi-skilled milk, and so on. So, the most expensive, and probably one of the nicest cheeses you can get, is made using double cream. For my taste, the cheap one is fairly bland. It was frequently used as Breakfast cheese when we stayed in hotels during our early days visiting Turkey.

Kasar cheese was similar to Edam, and this was my go-to cheese for making sandwiches for the boys.

Back then, I needed to learn quickly. Breakfasts can become boring for small boys. I couldn't find boxes of cereal, and a full English was just a dream. No sausage, no bacon, no beans! Eggs were plentiful and I was surprised how yellow they were when I first used them. Boiled, fried, poached and scrambled, with or without cheese were all popular. But how small boys become quickly bored.

I was lucky that my landlord lived in the same building, with his elderly sister. During the years we lived in the same building as them, she was a great help. Now, check this breakfast out. First of all, I was advised to be at the Friday morning market really early, so at 6am I was there. I bought milk off one of the old ladies who came down from the mountains to sell whatever they had grown, cultivated or produced from their livestock. Their milk was normally sold in cola bottles. I didn't think about the fact that it wasn't pasteurised, Turks had been buying it for years after all.

I took the milk home, put it in a big open pan and boiled it. I boiled it for several hours, then turned the heat off, covered it over and left it to cool. OK, step one done. Super breakfast on its way boys. Step two. Once the milk was cold, I used a slotted spoon and scooped off the cream from the top of the milk. The milk was put in a jug and used as normal milk. The cream was put in a bowl and put in the fridge. It was stored overnight. Next morning, I was up very early. A walk to the baker's where I asked for two bread doughs. Basically, for the same price as a baked loaf, I received a dough. Well, two. Once home, I set out the table as normal with juice and teas, crockery cutlery and my cream from the previous day with a jar of shop-bought strawberry jam.

Then, my magic. I oiled my hands and broke off the dough into pieces and rolled them into small balls in my hands. Then I flattened the balls and dropped them one at a time into clean hot oil that I'd turned on to heat up earlier. A slotted spoon, a few minutes bubbling away, and I had something like a doughnut. The smell had woken the boys, who came wandering into the kitchen asking what I was doing. I put the 'doughnuts' onto the table, and with the cream, the jam and lots of juice, we had an amazingly successful breakfast!

Over the next few years, I learned to pickle onions and red cabbage. I made my own lemon curd. I failed miserably with jam, but that was readily available in the shops. I put peaches into brandy in the summer to use at Christmas. Once my Mum and Dad moved there, I even made my Dad a 'pork pie' with my own handmade water pastry and gelatine. With not a bit of pork anywhere in sight! Dad loved it. I learned how to bake. Fruit cakes, carrot cake, Christmas cake. I made jam tarts, lemon tarts and I even made my own Christmas mince so we could have mince pies.

I became familiar with the spices and varieties of nuts, figs, dates, and of course, pistachios.

I made meat pies; I had turned into Mrs Beeton!

For the first time in my life, I used spinach, and we all loved it. I made courgette omelettes, and aubergines with yoghurt and tomato salsa. I even made borek, which is rolled up in a round tin.

I learned Turkish techniques of cooking but managed an English outcome. The boys were happy. Their diet was a healthy, mixed one. But making breakfast just wasn't as easy as opening a box ever again!

I was lucky, and over the years, friends, family, or my customers in my Property Management business who become friends, would bring out European foods for me. The one thing I just couldn't do without was gravy mix, but come on, I am from Yorkshire.

Over the years it's certain to have become easier, due to the number of tourists visiting and people moving to Turkey to live. But I'm sure it's still not easy. However, you guys living over there have access to some of the freshest, healthiest and fabulous fruit and veg. You lucky things!

Whilst I'm talking about not having European food, I remember when I lived there that the expats would have little get togethers whenever we brought back, or had been brought back by someone, something 'special'. Now special might not mean the same to you and me. But for me, 'special' was being given a jar of instant gravy, or a jar of Branston Pickle. Marmite wasn't on my list, but some of the girls loved the horrible stuff, and lived for the day it would appear for them. We would have a Branston pickle party, we would have a Marmite party!

I remember distinctly that I had a sneaky bacon sandwich, and that it was the best sandwich I have ever eaten. It did make me feel guilty, however, when I left my apartment that day (and the next). A lot of people in the block asked me what I had been cooking. They said it smelt so lovely! Oops!

There was another drawback. At the time I was still trying to bring the boys up as Muslims. I had tried to read as much as I could of the Koran, but it was way too difficult for me. The boys' father was neither interested, nor very religious, so I was struggling. A while after the 'Bacon Sandwich Incident' I sat the boys down and basically told them that the 'Pig Police' that I had been scaring them with for years would come for me if they told anyone. I know that scaring them hadn't been a good thing to do, but living in England with pork everywhere was incredibly difficult to cope with. I'd had to inform the school they weren't to eat it; I'd had to stop friends, family and neighbours giving them things that had pork in them.

The way that things were starting to happen in our lives, I eventually decided that religion isn't the real thing to worry about. Good morals, kindness and having a thought for each other was. I sat the boys down one afternoon and told them that I would leave the decision entirely up to them as to which religion they considered themselves to belong to. Provided that they grew up to be the best they could be, I would no longer interfere. They turned out great, and I never interfered again.

Back to my neighbours, though. Just about every year that I lived in Turkey, I would spend time making Christmas foods. My own cake, tarts, yule logs etc. One of my most popular for the family was mince pies, made with my own hand-made mince. My neighbours had all been so kind all year. Babysitting, providing food when I arrived home after a hard and long day at work, and offering help and advice. I decided one year that I wanted to give back something particularly English. I worked hard one morning making lots of mince pies. All nicely decorated with a scattering of icing sugar, and all nicely displayed on lovely paper plates I'd bought for them. I delivered the mince pies and said Thank you for all their help that year. I also went to the trouble of ensuring it wasn't done as part of our Christmas festivities.

Over the next few days, I received a lot of good comments regarding my mince pies. A couple of the ladies asked for the recipe. It was then that I realised I would be struck by lightning on my next trip outdoors. I started to copy and translate my mincemeat recipe. I was just between the list of ingredients and the how-to part. The part where you need to soak the fruit in alcohol! Muslims don't touch alcohol. This was especially true for the ladies living in my apartment block. I never told anyone.

I clearly didn't get struck by lightning, but I did feel guilty for quite a while afterwards!

Shopkeeper of the Year?

Way back when I lived in Alanya, I saved hard to purchase a rather expensive pair of leather shoes with laces that fastened around the leg. You know the style, like posh espadrilles. Anyway, I bought these shoes and was looking forward to wearing them to go out that same evening. I had planned to join a girls' night out. Although I'm a big bird, I do consider that I have reasonably good legs, and I loved shoes, so I was very happy with my purchase, and I went back to work. I was working in a restaurant at the time. I left the shoes in their box inside the shop carrier bag and continued to work until my time was up.

I dashed home, eager for my night out. I showered, dressed, put my make-up on and I took my precious, and rather expensive (for me) purchase from their box. I slipped them on and strapped them to my legs. But ohh! Before I had even stood up, one of the laces snapped.

OK. I still had enough time to go to the shop and change them before heading out with the girls. No major problems there then! I reached the shop and in my best Turkish, which wasn't too bad since I had already lived there for eight years, I explained that I had bought them earlier in the day. I hadn't even worn the shoes. It didn't take a rocket scientist to see that the bottoms of the shoes were as clean and unused as when I bought them. My bad luck, however, he doesn't have another pair the same size. But, he says, he can get them repaired fairly quickly if I want to wait. He even offered me a tea while I waited. OK, sounded reasonable to me. I agreed and I sat patiently and waited for my shoes to be repaired and returned.

My shoes reappeared quite quickly looking the same as they had when I bought them. I tried them on in the shoe shop. I dropped the shoes I'd worn to get to the shoe shop off at work, so that I didn't have to carry them about with me. I continued on to join my friends on our night out. But noooo! Second disaster, several hours into our night out, the bloody lace snaps again! The same one. I'm gutted. I'm absolutely gutted, and now I'm limping. And my street cred, if ever I had any, has just gone out of the window as I limp about. I decided to call it a night then, as all the fun had gone from my evening. I headed home in a taxi, as I was struggling with my shoe, and I had the bit of lace in my handbag. I threw myself into bed and had nightmares of my shoelaces strangling me.

The next morning, I get the shoes, and the lace, and I am determined to head off back to the shop to retrieve my hard-earned cash. These shoes were truly shite. I'd buy a different pair from somewhere else. But as I look carefully at the lace, it's not leather. The original lace was leather, but just seemed dry, which is why I thought it had snapped. This lace has little copper wires sticking out of the end of it. What the hell? It also seemed slightly stretchy. Odd, how very odd!

Anyhow, befuddled, beguiled and angry, I head off to the shop. Its Saturday, and it's busy. I begin to explain to the shop keeper that bearing in mind I had been patient, but because the same lace had snapped twice, I would like a full refund. I had only bought them the day before! I wasn't happy with them at all. Don't forget as you read this, that I had also spent many weeks saving up to buy them. Then I remembered to ask why the lace had wire sticking out of it?

The shop keeper starts to explain that, as I was fat, (cheeky sod, he wasn't exactly Paul bloody Newman), and that because I had snapped the first lace, he thought that it would be better to repair my rather expensive shoes with telephone cable! He seemed to have forgotten that I hadn't even worn the shoes when the first lace snapped. The sheer bloody nerve of this pleb. We then got into rather a heated argument about fat birds and the quality of his stock. This was partly in Turkish and partly in English. We were gathering a few spectators by now. Apparently, it seemed that he thought, in his wisdom, that I was too big to buy and wear the kind of shoes we were arguing about.

To cut a very, very long argument short, the shop keeper was refusing to give me back my hard-earned cash. He wanted me to take a different pair of shoes. Ones obviously designed with fat ladies in mind! They were both boring and very old fashioned, and or course everyone knows that over-weight people are also both old fashioned and boring….. Ha, I don't think so!

Needless to say, in my own inimitable way, I threatened to boycott his shop. I would put posters on his windows explaining that if you were fat, you shouldn't shop there. I threatened to walk up and down outside his shop every day, telling all the fat people who were looking at his stock that they should continue walking past and find a fat-friendly shop keeper. Looking back that might have been a little excessive, but I would have done it. I worked incredibly hard for everything I had and had saved hard for what I considered a little luxury for myself. He was fighting a battle that he could not win!

Eventually, he gave me my money back. I went to another shop and bought a similar type of shoe which were actually a little cheaper. I was still wearing them many, many months later without any incidents.

In the myriad of absolutely outstanding shop keepers in Alanya, people who would haggle, who would joke, but who would also ensure that you were happy with what you bought, I had managed to find the one rude, very stupid, very prejudiced shopkeeper who certainly wouldn't get my vote as Shopkeeper of the Year!

Snakes!

I didn't really consider that there might be snakes in Turkey when we all moved out there. But I can tell you with confidence that there are! I have had the unfortunate experience to meet not one but two of these things.

You know I'm planning to tell you, so be aware if you don't like them!

My first, and looking back the funniest, encounter was in the height of summer in Alanya. It was so hot and humid, which made it really difficult to work. At the time I was running a small, but fairly successful, property management company. I was looking after several apartments and a couple of villas belonging to my customers, most of whom were Irish. I was heading up to one of these villas, which was perched high on one of the hills overlooking Alanya. I was, and still am, fairly tight with money. That day, even thought it was incredibly hot, I had all the windows open and was surviving with the draught rather than using extra fuel running the air conditioner.

Imagine if you will, on the right side was a field with something tall in, I am tempted to say it was like cane. I really don't know, but it was tall. On the other side of the narrow lane that I was travelling on there was a drop of a few metres down to another field. I was driving carefully, as the lane wasn't that good. I had been up there lots of times, and I was always worried about meeting someone else coming the other way, as there really was nowhere to go and nowhere to pass. Fortunately, I never did, but I did meet something far worse.

This particular day, my music was on, windows open and I was concentrating on the road when suddenly out of the corner of my eye I saw the biggest, fattest snake, slithering out of the tall cane field. Now it was right in front of my car! I did something that makes me laugh whenever I think of it.

First, I sharply jammed my brakes on. Then I let out a blood curdling scream, the likes of which I have never made before, or even heard before. I was shuddering! You know what I mean, that thing you do when you are faced with something that makes your skin crawl. The snake had stopped right across the lane in front of me. It was brown and massive, almost the full width of the lane. And it was fat. Boy it was fat. I was still squealing as I closed all my windows and locked the doors. Goodness knows what I thought the bloody thing was planning to do, but looking back I hardly think that it was planning to rise up and come through my window, and even less likely to rise up, open the door and come in and swallow me whole. At the time though, that did seem like a possibility.

I stopped squealing since I was now locked in and safe. But the snake was just lying there in front of the car. What should I do? I was really not prepared to leave the safety of my car and try and shoo it off the road with my cardigan. Besides, I didn't have a cardigan! I was having a standoff with a snake. Was it poisonous? Did it have a large family to support that might have been waiting to ambush me? Were snakes protected by law? Would I be breaking the law if I squished it? Could it be squished? It was massive and seemed to be getting bigger every minute.

I sat there for what seemed like hours. I was absolutely sweating and red hot. I had, in my terror, forgotten to turn the air conditioning on. I'm really not sure in reality how long I was sitting there, too scared to move, too scared to get out of the car and see what I could do. I didn't really want to try and reverse down the lane. It was a long way, and in my fear, I might have found the fastest route down the hill. In other words, off the lane and away down over the fields!

OK, only one thing to do. I had to run it over! Perhaps if I set off slowly and kind of nudged it, it might just slither off down the hill. But, as it happens, it turned out to be as stupid as the pigeons that I regularly run over on my way to work these days. I work in a small village and start work very early. On these early mornings in the summer, there are always dozens of pigeons sitting on the road. I've tried honking my horn, flashing my lights, slowing down, but I refuse to swerve and risk an accident, so I regularly run them over. Not by choice, but because they appear to be too stupid to move, or maybe they are committing suicide?

I put my car in gear and moved forward. No movement from my adversary, but I was not prepared to get out and shoo it, No, no, no and no. I drove further forward, then I felt the same sort of feeling you get going over a steep speed bump. I was absolutely freaking out and had started making funny squealing noises. I felt the back wheels make the same bump and I drove further forward. First in the door mirror, and then through the back window, I saw it partially squished and now wriggling about. For a split second I felt sorry for it. I felt bad, it was just going along in its daily business. But why didn't the stupid thing just slither off down the field?

I reversed and ran it over again, then once more pulled forward and ran it over a third time, just to be safe. It had stopped moving after the third pass. I continued up to the villa that was looking after, jumped out of the car, ran up to the door, quickly unlocked it and went in. I did what I needed to as quickly as I could and was swiftly back in the car heading back down the hill. When I reached Mr Slippy, I ran him over again, just to be sure.

I did feel bad for a while afterwards but what else was a girl to do?

The following season, I was again driving somewhere. I had both my boys in the car with me. I can't remember where we were going, but I do remember we were on another narrow lane that wound around the back of Alanya. Driving down the road, we were approaching a park on the left-hand side. It was a green park that also had some kid's equipment, and there were a few kids enjoying the cooler evening we were having that day.

Once again, a big snake came rolling out of the side of the road heading across the road towards the kids' park. Big, although not as big as Mr Slippy. This time there was no hesitation. I was in a position to potentially save many kids from being squeezed to death, or consumed, or both! So, I ran straight over the pigging thing! Bish bash bosh. Then I stopped reversed and ran it over again then I continued my journey by running it over a third time.

My kids were freaking out due to the size of it. But they were also impressed. They knew nothing of my run in with Mr Slippy up the hill, and I had made tackling this enormous beast seem easy!

I'm sorry if there are people reading this who love snakes and feel I was acting over the top, but the first one was stupid and just wouldn't move. The second? Well I think I saved lives that day!

The Biggest Catch and a Clean Octopus

I have seen and done some mad things in my life, some mad dangerous, some mad funny, and some just downright 'mad'. This little story is a downright mad one that I got caught up in, and I'm not really sure how I got caught up in it.

When we lived in Turkey, my boys were super keen fishermen. When they were old enough, at weekends and during the long school holidays, (they have 13 weeks off in the Summer in Turkey), they would head off to the harbour. On their none fishing days, their growing collection of fishing tackle was stored on the balcony of their bedroom. It did turn into somewhat of a no go zone for me, it was way too dangerous as they left everything in a heap when they got home and that could include unused bait, which in the heat of Turkey would be way too scary to approach. Hooks of every shape and size, line which would entrap you, and fishing rods of various styles. They were lucky as some of the Irish customers of my little property management company would bring fishing rods, reels and all sorts of tackle out for them. Some of the rods became so cherished that they would take pride of place on the balcony and were never to be touched by anyone else.

So, after way too many arguments with the boys, I gave up cleaning the said balcony, with the agreement that they would keep it clean themselves. Surprisingly, they did. I put a small table and two chairs out there, and it became their space. They would sit for hours when the mood was on them, and clear up, pack up and sort out all their tackle. They would do whatever it's called when you fasten the line to the rod, and they would fasten hooks, floats and weights on. They loved it. If you have read the Fat Bird before this one, you'll know about the fishing competition, the friends they had. The Turkish friends who helped keep them safe. I'm happy to say my eldest son has continued with his love of fishing and even today will regularly turn up when he's on leave from the Army with his tackle and spend the day out fishing in all weathers.

I would give them a small amount of cash so they could buy bait on their way down to the harbour together with a packed lunch, and they were out for the whole day. Safe, out in the fresh air and with lots of friends. They have, over the years, told me lots of stories, but there are two that I witnessed which I want to share.

The first is a tale of karma, and I love karma. Neither of my kids liked my ex husband very much, but he didn't like them either. I really would not have remarried if I knew that this dislike would emerge. My kids are worth 1000 times more than any man, but at the time of my wedding I didn't know, didn't sense it, maybe I was temporarily blind but hind sight is, as they say a wonderful thing.

But, as I say, Karma is truly a bitch, and love her or hate her, she is there, lurking in the corner, ready to jump out and do her stuff. One particular day, the boys were already out fishing in the harbour area. Mum and I had decided to take a walk down to see them and have a drink at a lovely little café called, appropriately, 'The Fisherman's Café'. It's since changed but in those days, it was situated on the edge of the harbour, partly in the open air, with a covered section next to the bar further back from the road. They served drinks and light snacks and it was a nice place to sit, meet friends or just watch the world go by. I did, in the years I lived in Alanya, spend a lot of time there, it was a great place to sit and watch the boys fishing.

Alanya Harbour is a big place, and this end of the harbour was, I'm reliably informed a good place for catching Octopus! I did hear, not at the time it was happening but over dinner times when both boys are home on leave and in the mood to tell stories, that many Octopuses or is it Octopi, more than one anyway, had been battled with then finally captured, and then taken to the fish market and sold! I had two budding entrepreneurs even back then!

This day, Fikret, my ex-husband said he'd come with us, and we all set off on a nice steady walk down to the harbour. The boys weren't aware that we planned to turn up, in fact Mum and I had only just decided a few minutes before we set off. As we walked down the harbour side towards the café, I could see the boys, laughing and chatting and walking up and down for a few yards on the harbour side. I love my boys and the sight of them just blissfully happy always made me smile and still does.

But as they caught sight of us, there smiles disappeared. I knew that it was because they had seen Fikret, there was always an air when the three of them were together. He would never, and I mean never, tell them they were doing well, that they had done something cool or clever, or that they looked good if they were dressed up for some occasion. But he was always ready to put them down or outdo them. I would stop him every time I saw him putting my kids down in any way, but I know he did it when I wasn't there. He was a big kid himself!

I asked the boys if they wanted something to eat or drink, and they both asked for a drink and a toastie. The café was designed in such a way that the edge of the café ran along the side of the harbour and there was, if I remember correctly, just a low wall between the undercover part of the café where we were seated and the harbour. So, the boys just moved their belongings and continued fishing as their toastie was put together. We all chatted, and they had Mum and I laughing as they told us about the ones that had got away that morning.

They came to sit with us for a couple of minutes whilst their toasties were hastily consumed, and the drinks never even touched the sides on the way down. They really didn't have the time to stop. But as the boys climbed back over the wall, Fikret asked Kaan, my youngest, to give him his rod, as he intended to show Aslan how to fish! Kaan wasn't very happy, but I said it was only for a few minutes. Aslan was clearly amused and not fazed by Fikret's comment at all.

This may be one of those stories where you really needed to be there, but I'll try my best. Now, just to set the scene, there are a lot of little fishing boats bobbing about a few yards from the café, but if you cast properly, as the kids were clearly able to do, there were many fish to be had and they had caught lots there in the past. Aslan, taking no notice of Fikret whatsoever, cast his rod and stood smiling at me, with a knowing look, as he knew as well as I did that Fikret had never cast a rod in his life. He had often said that fishing was a fool's game and a waste of one's time.

Fikret had taken Kaan's rod and climbed over the wall, so he too was now at the harbour side. He swung his rod back ready to cast, and at that exact moment caught the biggest fish ever. He really had! The ceiling of the café was covered in fishing nets, hung in unattractive swags, and fastened to said swags was a collection of everything fishy, ranging from shells, pebbles, corks and floats, to tiny dried turtles and dried fish of many, many different types and sizes. You got the picture now?

Fikret had, without his line even touching the water, hooked onto probably the biggest, ugliest dried fish fastened onto the café fishing net ceiling swags! Kaan had by now collapsed with the comedy in front of him. Aslan stood grinning so broadly but was able to control himself quite admirably, Mum had let out a very loud 'OOhhhh' and me? Well I laughed. I laughed so much I think I actually came close to wetting my pants. I continued to laugh as the staff in the café had to use a chair to climb up and unhook Fikret's catch from his line. I laughed as Fikret started explaining that Kaan's rod was wrong, or the place they were fishing from was wrong, or that the sky was too blue and basically anything that would explain why he hadn't be able to show Aslan how to 'do it'!

I saw Karma standing next to Fikret and continued to laugh as Mum started making fun of him. Aslan had held it in as long as he could. He now exploded with laughter as the fish was unhooked. He had his say by asking Fikret if he wanted the man in the café to throw it back or put it in his keep net! Fikret surely had shown Aslan how to 'do it'. Fishing was rarely discussed by Fikret again!

Another story that springs to mind was when I was working at a friend's restaurant and the boys would walk there from the harbour and wait while I finished work so we could walk home together. The owner of the restaurant was a nice guy, and he would regularly get the staff to give the boys some of the staff food which was always a good meal. The story begins one evening when the boys turned up at the restaurant, very animated and chattering to each other. They were carrying a large shop carrier bag and presented me with it. I opened the bag and was totally, and I mean totally, grossed out at the sight of the ugliest face of an octopus staring up at me. Aslan was quick to explain that it was dead, and it was, it turned out, the first Octopus they had caught.

To digress slightly, they had always been transfixed when their Dad, Erkan, who had been a commercial scuba diver when we met, told them the story of him trying to catch a very large octopus when he was underwater. The octopus had fought back, covered his mask and grabbed his head whilst the battle ensued. As Erkan was explaining this to the boys, he would always make them jump by grabbing their heads as he told them his heroic story. But never did I ever imagine I would have one sitting on my lap.

Aslan explained they had brought it home so that they could have it for dinner! I coughed a little, stuttered a lot and explained that I really had no idea how to cook octopus. But they ahead of me already. The guys on the harbour side had told them that they should bang it on the floor until the ink was gone, which Aslan had done. Kaan did a pantomime to show me how Aslan had swung it round, seemingly hundreds of times, bashing it on the floor. Each time the black ink would spurt out. He did this until the ink stopped spurting.

The guys working in the restaurant were clearly impressed that my little kids had managed to bag their own dinner and they volunteered to cook it for them. Of course, the boys thought this a wonderful idea, so the octopus was carried away into the kitchen. The boys went into the kitchen to see what was happening and I continued with my own work, since it was some time before I could finish. About thirty minutes later the boys came out of the kitchen and the restaurant staff ushered them to a table and seated them like they were 'real' customers. Serviettes were provided, cutlery, a salad and some bread were put on the table. They were laughing and enjoying every second. Then the piece-de-resistance appeared on a big plate and was placed in front of them! The biggest pile of steaming octopus I have probably ever seen. A sight that I'm not particularly bothered about seeing again! In my opinion, the Octopus as a species had been on the top of the ugly tree and when it fell, it hit every branch on the way down. There is nothing attractive about it, from its ugly little face with a beak, to its weird sucker legs finishing with a sack of black ink. However, the boys thought it was a feast fit for kings, and they got stuck into it. I was asked if I would like to try it, but I wimped, I have eaten and enjoyed well-cooked calamari before, but I struggle to eat things that I wouldn't stand on! At least with the calamari, the origin of the animal was disguised. This octopus looked like an octopus.

To this day, I don't really know if the boys enjoyed the octopus. Their faces didn't give any clues, but knowing what they're like, they really couldn't have let me know if it was awful, since they wouldn't have heard the end of it from me. The guys in the restaurant had also gone to great lengths to cook the horrible thing. They claimed it was good, but they did seem to drink a lot with their meal, and when we got home, they both claimed to be very tired, and they went to bed early that night.

Before we left the restaurant, one of the chefs came out and was chatting with the boys and happened to tell them that the best thing they should do when they caught another was take it home and ask me to put it in the washer on a spin cycle. That way, the ink would come out and the machine would soften the animal up before it was cooked! Ha, yeah right! Never knew if they were setting us all up or not!

Two weeks later, there I was sitting in my kitchen, watching the head of an octopus hitting the door of my washing machine as it whizzed past. The noise of it banging the glass was something I shall never forget. The boys taking a shower as this was happening, and they were laughing. Yes, I bet they bloody were! How I had gotten into this I don't know. When the machine had finished, the octopus was removed, lovely and clean, it was beheaded and I pulled out what looked like organs and the ink sac, now empty. I then placed it in a large pan and boiled it. I actually had no idea what I was doing! It was served to their highnesses, and this time I knew it was not the nicest thing to eat. I know this because the following day I found lots of Octopus in the bin, and when the culprits were questioned, they admitted it was like chewing big rubber bands!

Never, will I ever rinse and boil Octopus again. That was a first and last!

Gazelle Lady

On one occasion Mum, the boys and myself were invited by Cevat for a visit to Osmaniye. I'd already been a few times, there was a great little hotel there which was very European. It's presence was always a mystery to me, because it was nowhere near the coast, and nowhere near any normal tourist routes. I once asked if it was owned or run by a European, but no, it was all Turkish. Bear in mind this was over twenty years ago, and in the East of Turkey. Things were different then.

Cevat had asked if Mum and the boys wanted to visit so that he could show them around. They were up for it, so it was all planned that, the next time I was out that way with Cevat, he would pay for the bus tickets to get them to Osmaniye and that we would meet them off the bus. I can't remember the exact length of the journey, but it was over twelve hours if my memory serves me right. Although Cevat had a large Mercedes, we thought that it was too far to travel with all five of us in it. We travelled during the night whenever we could, and sleep would have been impossible with everyone all squashed up. Anyway, the day when Mum and the boys were arriving came. Cevat and I had been in a factory close by to where we needed to meet them. I was learning about how people around the world were so complex when it came to buying grapefruits and oranges. Who would have thought! Some countries wanted them incredibly large, some wanted them small, even colour preference was discussed. I was really stunned by this, but it was important to the growers, who were trying to grow the fruit that would be easiest to sell.

The coach Mum and the boys were on was due to arrive at a local town called DortYol, and we set off to meet them. I loved that area of Turkey; Osmaniye, Erzin (where Cevat's business was based), Iskenderun and the capital of Hatay province, Antakya, which was ancient Antioch. These places were an odd mix of the old with the very modern, which I could never get my head around. The Hotel was The Osmaniye, right on the main street. It was modern, European in both style and service. Yet when you stepped outside it was very much the 'real' Turkey, nothing set up for tourists or foreigners at all. I got lots of stares and lots of people interested in this fat bird foreigner, but I became used to it and started to just say Merhaba (Hello) to them, and it either stopped them staring or it made them ask me why I was there. I love most Turkish people and if you try and speak their language, they are normally incredibly hospitable, and frankly very pleasant. Iskenderun was the same, old style buildings, parks, the shops were Turkish shops, no tourist shops and certainly no fakes to be seen anywhere.

Talking about this region again also reminds me about my ability to fall with style. Well, it's a real crowd-pleaser, anyway.

Once, whilst in Iskenderun, Cevat was attending a meeting, and he'd given me the choice to go with him or not. It was very hot, and I said I'd rather not, so I went off exploring. An hour into my exploration I found and bought THE nicest pair of boots I've ever owned. They were in the window of a very old looking shop. But they were super modern, almost knee high, very high-heeled stiletto boots with slightly pointy toes. Everything that was, at that time in vogue back home. Reading this today I'm sure no one will understand just how modern they were at the time, but they were. What a very random find! I wore those boots a lot. In fact, I wore them until the heel snapped when I was on one of my alcohol-fuelled nights out. I got a foot stuck in some kind of a drain and went head over tit, in probably not the most elegant fall I've ever made. Although both falls were in my younger days, and during my alcohol-fuelled break-down season, I did practice a lot!

My falls usually came about because, when I'd had a drink, I had this idea in my head that I'd turned into a gazelle, and I would start running! Inevitably, shortly after starting, I would fall down, no longer like the gazelle in my mind, more like a sack of potatoes being dragged about! Two falls come to mind, and now I've opened this door, I feel it's my responsibility to share them with you as we have our cup of tea. Are you ready?

The first memorable fall was many years ago, when I wasn't so vintage. On that occasion I was out with a few friends in Doncaster town centre. There were four of us, close friends, and we had so much fun every weekend. But well before we would arrive in Doncaster, we were normally smashed. This particular night was no different, except for the fact that I chose a very busy pedestrian precinct to do my impression of a gazelle. Set the picture, this was the age when fishnet tights were very 'in' and I had a pair on, with a knee length skirt and the other things that I really can't bring to mind. Anyhow, off I go, running down the precinct like a gazelle being chased by a leopard. With the voices of my friends in my ears, shouting and begging me to stop before I fall. Ha, too late! off I go on my way to headbutt the pavement. My friends caught me up, absolutely howling and saying things like, 'why do you always do that'? Well I believe it's because the wine back then wasn't made properly!

I got up, and I had hit my head. I mean, it's going to happen when you fall on the plains of the Serengeti and you're running from predators. I had also put two major holes in both knees of my fishnet tights. Basically, before the fall only tiddlers could have made it through that net, but afterwards, well, there was enough room for Nessie to get through! My knees were skinned badly, and when I tried to straighten myself up, I had skinned both the palms of my hands! This time I had seriously excelled myself.

I spent the rest of our evening feeling sorry for myself, and the next morning and day was spent hiding the skinless parts of me, and the bump on my forehead, from my parents. In my defence, I was only about nineteen, and I did, and still do, like to entertain everyone. My friends certainly thought it was amusing.

I did often wonder though, that if I could have been given wine before the PE lessons at school, whether I would have achieved far more. Particularly in the summer, when those horrible lines were painted onto the grass. I might even have run like a gazelle all the way round.

Coming back to Turkey, my second most impressive fall was in Osmaniye, where we would be staying with Mum and the boys. It was on a different trip there with the boys, when we'd gone out to a friend's engagement party. On this occasion, the boys and I came out of the hotel, directly onto the pavement of the high street. Out in that part of Turkey, whenever I was with the boys, we received even more interest, as the boys clearly looked Turkish but we were all chatting away in an Eh-by-gum accent. When I travelled out that way, I always tried to remain respectful and always wore clothes that covered me up. I've never been one to show my bits, but I tried harder when I was in the East. This day, I had a pair of black jeans on, with a black tunic, which was high necked, long sleeved and over the bum long. I rarely ever used a head covering, unless Cevat told me I was going to meet someone really religious, or we were going somewhere where there would be lots of covered women.

On this fateful day, we all stepped out of the hotel and walked a few yards down the road. We had only planned to just wander around to see what was what. Back then, and I guess even now, some of the pavement curbs in Turkey were abso-bloody-lutely enormously high. I'd been told a couple of different reasons for this. Who knows which is the truth, maybe both? One reason, I'd been told, was that many years ago it was designed to prevent drunken drivers running pedestrians over. The other was that it was to prevent the water flooding over the pavements during heavy rain. I know which I'd prefer to believe, and in my mind, I see lots of drunks bumping along the curbs on their way home.

We got to one of these bastard high curbs. Even on a good day, they aren't good for fat people. It's not like you can just step off and take it in your stride. Well, I have never been able to, anyway. I had developed a technique where I would stop and manoeuvre myself so that I could carefully put one foot down whilst leaning on my other leg, hoping it wouldn't buckle. Then I'd put the second leg down, which made me feel kind of smug. Although it wasn't elegant, it was an effective technique.

However, remember that on this particular occasion I've already got people watching me and the boys, wondering what we are all about. This step was much, much higher than my left leg was able to deal with. Once again, I was heading south to kiss the tarmac. I remember letting out a scream. In the circumstances who wouldn't? I hit the road, and I hit it very hard since it was at lease fifteen meters away. Well, it felt as if it was that high. I lay still for a few moments to just check that I hadn't broken anything valuable, you know, watch, ankle, knee, neck, that sort of thing. I could hear the boys asking me if I was OK and then trying really hard not to laugh as they helped me up. But, once I was upright, another problem came to light. Two problems really. One was that several people, actually a lot of people, including from across the road, had stopped what they were doing so that they could watch me. The second problem was that I was covered in something white. I never found out what the white stuff was. Was it road marking paint that I had rolled about in? I don't know, but I looked like I'd been dip dyed! The boys were by now past caring if I heard them laughing. They were in pieces, and I was hoping they'd pee themselves. Thankfully I hadn't gotten very far out of the hotel, so I was able to retreat back into my room and get changed, whilst giving the crowd outside time to disperse.

It was never mentioned again for a very long time!

Anyhow, I digressed again. Back to the story of Mum and the boys coming to Hatay on the bus. Hatay was, and probably still is, one of my favourite places in Turkey. Located on the border with Syria, it has an amazing history. From the Greeks to the Romans, through French and Syrian occupation, and now part of Turkey. It was known as Antioch, Antakya and then Hatay. St Peter visited there, and there is the church of St Peter which is set into a cave. The Museum of Hatay has some absolutely amazing Roman and Byzantine mosaics. I wouldn't recommend visiting right at this moment, but if the situation in that part of the world changes, then go. It's a fantastic place with fantastic people. Wander up the street where the soap shops are, you can go inside and see them actually making the soap. Amazing soap! People have used this as soap, shampoo and shower gel before there were showers. No one used plastic there!

Cevat and I met Mum and the boys off the bus, and we checked them into the hotel. We then headed out to explore. Cevat was pretty cool with the group of us, but he did tend to stick with the boys so he could talk to them. He showed us around for two days. He took us to some super restaurants and introduced us all to some food we had never tried, or even heard of before, and we had a fabulous time. He even took us to Harbiye waterfall. The love story of Apollo and Daphne was based there. It's a great place to visit in the heat of summer, to cool down around the bottom of the waterfall.

When it came to go home, I decided to travel back with Mum and the boys. Cevat and I had visited several fruit plants before they arrived, and now he needed to do some travelling around in the area, which I didn't want to do in the heat of the summer. Cevat went into the ticket office and bought our coach tickets, and when he came back, he explained that he had bought the whole back seat to give us a bit more room. We could pick the coach up in Osmaniye. So, off we went. Because we were travelling through the night, we had a light meal a couple of hours before we departed. We were hoping for a pleasant journey back to Alanya, with lots of sleep.

Ha! If anyone has ever travelled from Alanya, along the coast road, even as far as Anamur, you'll know how bad that road is. Not only is it twisty and turney, but it's up and down too, because it follows the coast the whole way. Add that to being seated at the back of a large coach. Well, it's the combination from hell, and none of us had thought it through. We left Osmaniye and within minutes we were on the worst road I have ever travelled on. Kaan was sitting next to me, and just as he said 'Mum, I don't feel well' he emitted the worst shower of projectile vomiting that I have ever had the misfortune to witness! Before I could do anything, he had covered the two rows in front of us, and the third row had caught some of the blast as well. Mum and I were horrified, Kaan had turned green, Aslan was feeling sick now and we were in Hell! The host on the bus rushed down to the back and gave us a couple of sick bags for the boys and a full packet of serviettes to clean Kaan up. He then turned his attention to the poor folk who had been in front of us, he cleaned them up and took a packet of biscuits away from one poor lady who had been eating them just as Kaan did the best impression of a volcano I have ever seen. The biscuits didn't escape the eruption either.

What made it worse for me was that every one of the people caught in this eruption, without exception, were so nice about it. They kept telling Kaan not to worry. They tried to make me feel better too, and generally just got on with cleaning themselves and the seats up. I did wonder if perhaps this happened a lot of this road? But It was THE longest coach ride ever, most of the people got off in Alanya with us. At one comfort stop, Mum and I bought lots of biscuits, some lemon cologne and more serviettes, and shared them out between these lovely understanding people. But it never made me feel better.

Never the back seat again, and I don't drink anymore, so the gazelle is extinct!

A dream In The Woods

On one of our adventures, the boys and I were in the area around Osmaniye and Erzin. We were attending the engagement party of a friend of mine, a lady called Carole Anne. The party was in my first book. During my visit, I met up with Ahmet, one of my favourite drivers with Airtours. He lived out there and was also big friends with the man that Carole Anne was becoming engaged to. Kismet, my other favourite driver, also lived close by, they all lived around there. They had all worked for the same bus company. After I started working with Cevat, I found out that it was actually his company that they had all worked for.

After the party, Ahmet asked me and the boys to go for a meal at his home the following day. We loved it. His Mum was lovely, and they were making their own style of Lavas/pitta bread/naan bread. I'm not sure what you should call it, but they were making it in the garden, in a specially made hole type oven lined with bricks. It was great to share this.

Ahmet told us that he wanted to show me and the boys something very special, and he truly did. After we made our farewells, we jumped in the car with him. This is a very long time ago, but I think we travelled high up above Osmaniye and into the forest. The boys were constantly asking where we were going but I had no idea, and Ahmet wasn't letting us into the secret yet. We stopped the car in an opening on the lane we had been travelling on for several minutes. We jumped out of the car and followed Ahmet. We followed him down an incline and then suddenly we all drew a breath. In front of us was the most amazing thing. It was a village with a little road and wooden houses on both sides. But there was no one there, not a soul, it was the spookiest place. Ahmet was delighted when he saw our reactions. We walked down the road. The houses were empty but not abandoned, some had been recently painted or touched up. All were in a good state of repair, some clearly very recent. No broken windows or broken doors, everything looked locked up and secure. There were dozens of these houses!

Ahmet then explained to us about the village, the boys had to help with a little translation as we were talking about things that my vocabulary didn't cover. But he explained that these houses had been built by some of the people who lived in Osmaniye in order to live in during the very hot summer months, when it was too hot in the city. They would move wives, mothers, kids and pets up to this village, and the men would live in their homes in the city during the week and join them on a weekend. The houses had all been hand-made, without builders or massive equipment. The place was fascinating, it just looked as if everyone had just locked their doors and gone off to watch a football match, and were due back any minute.

It was like a shanty town out in the swamps of the southern US, without the swamps and alligators, although I guess there are a lot of creepy crawlies and bugs.

The boys were looking through windows, but I asked them not to, it seemed so disrespectful. Ahmet pointed out platforms high up near the tops of the houses and explained that in the summer these would be piled high with cushions and people would sleep there. No electricity, and seemingly no running water, but what a great place! They must have made it work, and it seemed they'd been doing this for many years, rebuilding and repairing the houses as necessary. It was getting towards Autumn when we visited, and everyone had moved back to the city. It was an odd, spooky place, but in the summer when it was full of mainly women and kids, it must have been a phenomenal place. I was so glad I got to see it.

I'd forgotten about this place, as I had with a lot of things until I started writing down all of my little stories. Someone wrote quite a bad review of my first book, saying they would have preferred more details, that it was rushed, and that I was self-indulgent. I can't help with the lack of detail, I do feel that if I pushed in more detail I would lose the snappy style that I write in, putting in extra detail just for the sake of it. I didn't rush anything, but I admit that I do go for it when I type. When I set off, I have an idea of the story or anecdote that I want to share and I just type away. I don't stop to check grammar or punctuation; my husband edits my stories and he tries to take care of that. But maybe she was right about the self-indulgence. That's the nature of telling your own stories.

When googling self-indulgent, you typically find something like:

> *Saying that someone is self-indulgent, means that they allow themselves to have, or do, the things that they enjoy very much.*

So yes, I'll admit that I started my writing journey because I had always felt that I had a book inside me. My life has been interesting, unplanned, but amazing. I have fallen into being yet another accidental author, and I will confess to being self-indulgent. I have enjoyed writing these books very much. I have remembered places that I'd sadly forgotten. I'd forgotten people who were part of my life for a long time, and you know, I think I'm old enough to deserve a little self-indulgence.

I've been to Syria, and I've seen and done things that I will never get to repeat in eastern Turkey. I made friends with people from all walks of life, and been welcomed into their lives, and I feel privileged to have been allowed into their worlds. I didn't take anything for granted, I never mocked, belittled or made fun of things that were downright foreign to me. They were interesting, these people were real Turks and I'm sad to say that living in a tourist resort I have seen the flip side of Turkish people. I didn't particularly like the Estate Agents, but I do understand about making a living and feeding your kids. I didn't always like all the guys in shops and bars who would constantly be picking up girls and women, taking them for all they could get, then a week, or two weeks later, picking up a different woman. But they were getting by. In their positions, wouldn't we all be tempted? And who is to say that the women involved in all this really cared? They were being flattered, romanced and looked after for a brief time before heading back to real work. A job they didn't like, perhaps? And rain!

Ahmet was a real friend to me, to the boys, and to Mum and my Dad when he was alive. I'm very proud to call him a friend. He did very well for himself, he married a few years later, had kids and the last time we touched base he was running a small bus company in Istanbul. One day we will catch up and maybe meet again, I'd love to meet his kids.

Turkish Jewellers

I share this story with you at the risk that you might think I am showing off, or that I am being seriously self-indulgent. I'm not showing off, but I guess I am being self-indulgent, as what I will share with you is another chapter that makes my life the book it is. Good bad or indifferent are all part of the recipe.

I know I'm biased, but I really think that, when purchasing gold or diamonds, you would need to go a long way before you will find a better source than a good Turkish Jeweller. My first experience was when I holidayed in Turkey in the mid to late 80's. Bodrum and Marmaris were where I holidayed, and my first impression of the jewellers there was mind blowing. I couldn't get my head around the fact that there were dozens of jewellers all on the same road, or in the same area of the bazaar. How did they make money when they were all so close?

I didn't like the fact that, way back then, all retailers were very pushy in some way or other. I just wanted to look in the window, and I said a hundred times that, if they had just let me look, they would probably have had more chance of me walking in and buying something. Nowadays they don't do it as much. It's not allowed, but there is always one who is desperate and won't give in.

My first gold was bought in Marmaris. But then I couldn't stop, and every time we went to Turkey, I would buy something. Whatever I could afford, anything, including little gold charms (these were way ahead of, and more sophisticated than, Pandora). I found out years later that these little charms were mainly used for Sunnet gifts, or they were fastened, along with a

Turkish eye, onto the back of baby clothing as good luck charms and presents. I also bought earrings and chains. I loved Turkish jewellery.

When my boys' father asked me to marry him, we were in Izmir and went off to the bazaar for an engagement ring. At the time I was totally unaware of the Turkish way of doing things. I mean, women get engagement rings. Men don't, do they? Maybe as a people, the Turks have since changed the way they do this, but I learned afterwards that the normal way to become engaged back then was to choose a narrower version of a wedding band. I had seen them in the shops without really considering what they were. The man and the woman both have one, and both wear them on their right hand instead of the left, in order to denote that they are engaged.

However, at the time I didn't know that. Erkan, the father of my kids, didn't know that I didn't know it! He was in for a considerable shock when we got to the jewellers. He had gone to a shop where he knew the owner, which was a smart move as there were hundreds of jewellers to choose from. I knew a little amount of Turkish when all this was happening. Erkan knew a small amount of English, but we had developed our own language which no one else understood. We were, on the whole, able to get by reasonably well. We were lucky in that his friend spoke a fair amount of English too.

We went into the Jeweller. Drinks were offered, accepted and sent for. Shortly after that a little man with a round tray swinging on handles appeared carrying them. I was seated underneath all the hot lights in the jeweller's and was blinded with the array of rings in front of me. Erkan and the owner had a conversation and then a tray of these 'thin wedding bands' was put in front of me. I was a bit non-plussed, as we were there to get an engagement ring, weren't we? I did sort of brush these rings away, and when I think back, Erkan and this guy must have wondered what I was doing. But I was doing my own thing it seemed to them. And I was in a jeweller's, and doing it very well, and I picked out a few rings that were more of an Engagement ring style!

Looking back, Erkan and his friend passed a few comments to each other and it must have gone something like this, I guess. 'What the feck is she doing?' That would have been Erkan. 'I'm not sure mate, but if we can't steer her away from these rings, can you pay weekly?' Oh dear, what a predicament for him!

We were in that shop for a very long time. But several drinks later, and after a lot of effort getting to understand each other, we had decided that a ring would be made for me. I had kind of tacked two different rings together, and the owner had sketched me a ring design that I loved. It's difficult to explain, but it was like an arm which went round my ringer with a hand at the top which had a tiny ruby on its wedding finger. It was unusual. In my opinion it was a good buy for Erkan, as it didn't have any big stones in it. For years afterwards people would comment on it. In my defence though, I did ask how much it cost. They wouldn't tell me. I asked if I could help pay for it, but at that time Erkan loved me and he said NO, to this day, I don't know what it cost.

I discovered, a very long time afterwards, that Erkan did end up paying for my ring in instalments, but I'm worth it, aren't I? As I type this I'm laughing out loud, I was being sarcastic there.

Back to that bitch that is Karma though. Many years later though, and those of you who have read my first book will know the story, when Erkan and I were falling to pieces and our relationship was almost at its end, he stole my ring and sold it so he could continue gambling. So, he got the last laugh!

Once I was living in Alanya I had very little spare money for anything, least of all jewellery, and I was saddened when I was guiding and I would see some of the beautiful jewellery that guests had bought. They sometimes asked me to go into shops with them to help, and I was happy to. But boy it was hard when I didn't really have a pot to piss in.

A few years after my divorce from Erkan, I had met Fikret, a guy from Izmir. After a few months he asked me to marry him. Looking back, I should not have married him, but for lots of reasons, most of which were probably wrong, I agreed to become his wife. At the time I was running a very small property management business, and for the first time I was on my feet. I was paying my rent a year in advance so that I knew the boys and I were safe. I had managed to buy a Renault Kangoo, so I could ultimately make more money from airport transfers and from my day-to-day job of arranging furniture purchases, electricity supply, banks, insurance etc for my customers. Life was getting easier for the boys and myself. Fikret had been a personnel manager in Izmir. He worked with me in my business, but he hated it. It was beneath him.

One afternoon, Fikret and I had been visiting my Mum and Dad. One of my Uncles, a man almost like my Mum's twin due to their closeness in age, and my Aunt were visiting. I remember Fikret telling them that he was taking me to get my engagement ring, and I could have whatever I wanted. My Aunty, Uncle and Mum and Dad were so impressed! But Fikret didn't mean it, it was said for some sick show. Once we got outside Mum's apartment, he made a clear point of telling me that he was only joking. I should have called it off there and then, but hindsight is a wonderful thing.

When we got to the jewellery shop that Fikret had chosen, conversations took place, and several trays were put in front of me. It was quick process. I knew what I liked, and I picked a lovely princess-cut solitaire. It was sized, and Fikret paid a deposit. He never said another word in the shop, other than to say to the shop owner that money wasn't an issue and we agreed to collect it the next day. However, once outside, Fikret told me how much he would be putting towards my ring! So, the choices I then had were to pay the balance myself, or turn around and go back into the shop and cancel the ring. I only briefly considered doing that, which would have been the best choice, but I think I was more concerned about explaining to my family.

I have looked back many times and wondered why my pride had stepped in just there and then and stopped me from making the right decision. Hell, I have no answer!

Now fast forward many years to my David asking me to marry him. This was done in the Bahamas with a craft fayre ring being used as a temporary engagement ring. The full details of my fabulous proposal are in the Amazing Life book, but I never explained about my trip back to Turkey to buy my ring. Well here it is…

Once we got home from our Bahamas holiday, we talked about the best place to buy my 'real' ring. It had been many years since David had bought jewellery, and for me, there was only one place, Turkey. OK so I'm biased, and I always will be. I believe that Turkish jewellery is fantastic, and if I was now planning to wear a new wedding ring and engagement ring, there was only one place I could think of to buy it from. We booked to go to Alanya for four days, and a few weeks later we were walking down the main road from our Hotel to the centre to look in shop windows!

Before I continue, you must understand that all my life I've been hardworking, I've always had to be careful with money and for a lot of my days I was the main bread winner. At the time, as we all do, I never really thought about it, I never really expected any more, I just got on with life as best as I could. But now, for the first time in my life, I was in a wonderful position. I was with a man who could look after me. A man who was smart and able to earn more than me, a man who had taken the pressure off me for the first time in my life. I didn't intend to slow down; I didn't intend to retire and sit at home. I would, and have continued to, work hard. But I was walking down a road in Turkey to buy an engagement ring. I was really in love, and this time I wouldn't have to pay for it myself or volunteer to pay half. I was so excited!

I had an idea what I wanted, and it was something completely different from the rings I'd had before. I did feel a little like Elsie Tanner, and for my younger readers, Elsie was a big character in Coronation Street, back when Ken Barlow ran about with shorts and socks on! She married several times, but for more information you would need to google her.

So, David and I look in a few shops. I'd not lived in Alanya for a few years, so I didn't really have any contacts in any of the jewellery shops any longer, and it was really potluck. The first one we went it had some nice rings and one that was put on my 'possible' list. David was great, he had patience and wanted me to be sure. The next shop we went it was just off the main road in Alanya, a few hundred metres from the Friday market. I'm happy to name it as Magic Guler. I stepped into heaven that day! The trick in these shops is to give as much information as you can regarding the style and features you are looking for. This way the guys in the shops can find you what you're looking for much quicker, if they are any good at what they do. Most of them are really good.

After giving us drinks, and tuning on the air conditioner, the guy in this shop sat and listened to what I had in mind. He came back to us with a couple of rings, both beautiful, one was more the style we were looking for. Further rings were brought out. Some fitted, some didn't, but we knew that they could be resized very quickly for me. By now there were a few rings in front of us. I had pushed a couple to one side, and they were put back into the shop window. The guy in the shop said something to one of the other men working in there, and that guy left the shop. He was going to another shop to fetch a ring for me to look at.

It was only at this point that I let the guy in the shop know that I actually understood a lot of what he was saying, and that I'd lived right there in Alanya for a long time. He laughed at me for keeping it secret, but I was just checking him out, I guess. Just to make sure there was no 'funny business'. I am from Yorkshire after all, and we don't like 'funny business'!

The man who had gone to another shop returned and put the most spectacular ring in front me. It was everything, and more, than I had imagined. I tried it on, expecting it to stop before it reached my knuckle, but no, it slid past my knuckle and fit me as if it had been made for me! I think David knew; I think my eyes must have shone. He asked the price. When I heard it, I almost yelped. I took the ring off and pushed it to one side. Further rings came out of the window, and I found another potential candidate. This time the price sounded a lot more reasonable.

David could sense I was getting to the point where I couldn't seem to make a choice so he announced that we would go for a drink and be back in about 30 minutes. Perhaps the guy in the shop thought we were just making a break for it, but we did actually go into the bazaar area and sit at one of our favourite bars and order a drink. David asked me what I thought. I gave him my views, but the most important one was that I trusted this Jeweller, and I liked the shop. He agreed and then he asked if what I really wanted was the ring that had been brought over from the other shop. I told him I loved it more than any ring I'd seen before, but the price was way too scary. He told me that was his problem, and that if I wanted it and if I would wear it without being scared, then I could have it.

I've shortened the conversation we had, of course. It was quite a long, backwards and forwards conversation, involving me making excuses not to buy it, and David making reasons why I should!

We finished our drinks and headed back to the shop. When we were in there earlier, the Jeweller had offered to reduce the cost by putting a smaller diamond in the ring I liked. David and I had also discussed this option. We walked in and David said, we want that one and he pointed to THE ring, which had been moved from the countertop but was still there in the case underneath. The guy seemed surprised and asked what size diamond we wanted. David said, 'the one that's in it'! Phone calls were made to the sister shop where it came from, but I was too far away and couldn't hear the conversation. Bad news! The ring was sold to a German Lady and she was due to collect it later that evening.

Gutted didn't come close to how we felt. But then the Jeweller asked how long we would be in Alanya. We told him the day we were planning to leave. He then stunned us by stating that they could make one that was exactly the same for me, before we left. And they did! We picked the diamond size, they sized the ring, asked for the rings I was wearing so they could clean them. We also chose wedding rings to match, David paid a deposit, and it was done. We returned to the shop the night before we were due to leave the resort. My ring was there, a beautiful square halo ring. I slipped all my other rings back on, and then my engagement ring. I rarely take it off and I am the happiest woman in the world!

I hesitated about including this story, but I did it for a few reasons. First, I received a lot of comments about my first book, and some made it sound like they thought my life must over now I've left Turkey. No, it didn't end. I feel like it's just as amazing today, but now it's amazing in lots of different countries!

I also wanted to share with anyone who hasn't visited Turkey, that you should, if you are looking for jewellery, try a Turkish jewellery shop. Well worth the visit, I guarantee. Those guys know their job really well, they have patience to show you a hundred items if necessary, until you're sure. They will put the air conditioning on and organise a drink for you so you're not hot and bothered whilst you are choosing. They will get your item sized up for you, sometimes within an hour or so. They will normally offer to clean your own jewellery at the same time. And it's seriously good fun!

Also, to show that fat birds also find their knight in shining armour, be they Turks, Brits or men from Mars. We aren't there to mock, laugh at or call bubbly. We are a Force to be reckoned with!

Socks in the Snow!

During my time in Turkey I opened a small roadside tour business. You know the type, selling jeep safaris, boat trips, Turkish nights? Well we had bigger plans, but unfortunately due to war and terrorism they didn't happen. I won't go into it, it was a story in my first book, but we had planned to keep running during the winter months if we could. Because the year this business opened was an incredibly quiet year with a lack of tourists, Fehmi, the guy who was managing the tour business with me, suggested that we approach the local school to see if we could do anything with them. It did seem like a good idea at the time.

Fehmi and I made an appointment with the head of the school, and we had come up with an idea to take the kids to Saklikent, which is a ski resort close to Antalya. Quite a long trip, but doable. We thought it would be great to let the kids, most of whom would never have seen snow close up, to get to play in it and enjoy something they would normally only see from a distance during winter, when the Taurus mountains surrounding Alanya would be covered in snow.

I let Fehmi do the talking with the head, but I could understand most of what was being agreed. We had calculated a price per child, and I had already spoken with several of my English friends who had agreed to come with us as guides to ensure we didn't lose anyone. We left the meeting feeling good about all the plans We designed a few posters which were taken back to the school, and had given the head a couple of weeks to come up with numbers so we could organise the coaches. We thought we had covered everything. Little did we know!

So, fast forward to the day of the trip. We had been given numbers and two buses were ordered. We had checked, and Saklikent had a nice covering of snow. My friends were all ready to help out, and we were parked outside the school waiting for the kids to arrive. I had also brought with me a large number of plastic carrier bags. I really didn't want to be cleaning vomit up for the rest of the day. They would also come in handy for rubbish as the kids had been asked to bring a packed lunch and a little cash if they wanted a warm drink.

The kids started turning up, there seemed to be a lot of them, and when we started checking names, there were a lot of them! Way too many. Fehmi hadn't wanted to join us on the day, he wanted to keep the tour office open, but I called him to see where we might have gone wrong. He made a few calls and when he called me back, I was stunned! Apparently, a lot of the kids, or probably their parents, had decided at the last minute, long after we had been given the numbers. They had all said they would pay on the day. Fehmi did have the sense to call for an extra coach and it turned up a few minutes after I put the phone down to him. Luckily, being a tourist resort, there were lots of buses for hire around. OK, that was dealt with. I collected all the last-minute attendees' money and added them to our lists and we had enough seats for bums. I moved some of my friends about so there was a 'guide' on every coach. I could easily pay for the extra coach the following day, so we were on our way.

We didn't get far before there were lots of squeals on the bus I was on. When I went to the rear of the bus to find out what was happening, the kids had all moved to the side of the bus nearest the sea. If you ever travelled from Antalya to Alanya, you'll know the road. Many years ago, when I lived there, it was an open cliff sided coastal road. Today there are tunnels, and it is a lot safer, but back then it would, especially in the dark, be a bit hairy to travel on. The kids had seen something that I had never seen before and never seen since. Three waterspouts out at sea. These are high funnels of water, like a mini twister. I looked them up and read about them afterwards. They were impressive to watch as we travelled along, but a couple of the kids were freaking out, thinking they would be sucked up. We all watched in amazement, and at the same time I tried to calm the freaked kids. The waterspouts seemed to simply run out of steam, and slowly sank back into the sea. The kids were put back in their seats and we continued the trip.

We arrived in Saklikent and the sun was shining brightly. As we approached, we started to travel up a road with snow on the shoulders, and the kids were all shouting and loving it. That alone made it all worthwhile. We followed the signs and the buses pulled up, side by side in the car park. I climbed off and asked everyone to stay onboard until all my friends and I could sort out getting the kids off safely. My boys were with us, they went to the school, and had paid for their seats but they were my translators that day and were a big help.

My friends and I made plans how we would get the kids safely from the car park to the safe ' no traffic' area, and my boys passed the plan for moving and meeting back up again on to the kids. I had taken an umbrella I owned that had a large bright yellow sunflower on it. The plan was that I would put the umbrella up when it was time to eat, and then again when it was time to leave. We had seen in the brochures, and we'd spoken to people who had been there, about a seating area on a dry part of the complex. They could have their lunches there and grab a tea or soft drink if they wanted one. The drivers were fine with them leaving their food on the bus and collecting it at the time we agreed. Right we were all set!

With everyone in position, we started to let the kids off the buses. But wait, something was very wrong. Because of the little panic when we were putting them on buses, we hadn't noticed that some of the kids were wearing flip flops and a pair of brightly coloured socks! Oh my lord! We hadn't thought to warn parents that the kids would need wellingtons, or at least a strong full shoe. Some had wellingtons, most had a full sturdy shoe, but what could we do with the flip flop kids? I then remembered the huge amount of carrier bags I had with me, we had only suffered with one child being ill on the way there, so I had loads of them on the bus.

We ushered them all to a safe place, on tarmac but close to the snow and near the picnic tables. The kids with appropriate footwear were told they could go, but they needed to stay within a defined area. The flip flop kids were sat down and told to take off their socks. I think they thought we were all bonkers. We then put their feet into carrier bags and put their socks over the top. We told them that if they became too cold, to come back to us, but none did. But I remember playing out in the snow when I was small, Feet, hands, face… always freezing but way too much fun to give in.

They all came back to eat lunch and they all looked so cold but so happy that I bought them all a glass of tea. Little red faces smiling up and all chattering about the snow. What snow did if you did this and if you did that. How to make snowmen, which my boys helped them with.

When they went back to play, some had been given plastic sheeting and they were sitting on it and sliding down the hillside. Some were building snowmen, or just creating huge piles of snow. A couple had even got hold of a plastic sled, given, I'm guessing, by some wonderful tourist who saw all the kids playing.

At the end of the day, the umbrella went up. It had worked well at lunch time, but it seemed to be taking an age for them all to turn up this time. We counted them in slowly and it was then that I noticed some of them digging what seemed like rubbish out of the bins! What on earth? They then disappeared again. When they finally returned and joined the queue to be counted back in, they had bottles, plastic bottles of every description, small to very large. They had filled them with snow! When I asked what they were doing, bless these kids, they explained that they wanted to take some snow back to show their parents and siblings! I tried to explain that the heating would be on in the bus because we were all so cold and wet, and that when they got home they would just have a bottle of dirty water, but they wouldn't believe me. They thought I was joking with them. How could that wonderful fun white stuff change into dirty water? The bus drivers all tried to stop them getting on the buses with these treasures, but they really, really wanted to take them home, so the bus drivers gave in and eventually just stood screwing the bottle tops on firmly so we had no leaks!

All on the buses, all accounted for, heating on so they could dry out their socks and feet, not one of them complained. A lot of them had gone off to sleep very quickly, then bugger me, one of the buses broke down coming down the mountainside. What now? Karen, my friend on that bus called me to say the bus had just stopped, wouldn't restart, what should they do? We had stuck close together and there were empty seats after we had engaged the third bus, so we went back to them and I called and asked the third bus not to pass them, but to stop. We moved the kids off the casualty bus, and although they were a little cramped up with three on a seat in places, we did it. The driver of the broken-down bus called his company to get help, we continued onwards and eventually, after a day that had lasted three weeks, we arrived back in Alanya. We were a little later than planned, but lots of parents were waiting there to receive back. Their little ones and a bottle of dirty water!

Despite the problems, the socks, the snow, the breakdown and the extra kids, we had all had a fabulous time. From my point of view, even though it was business, watching these kids and being privileged to be with them when they saw snow close up for the first time, I will never forget that day. But never again did we, as a business, do anything with the schools again!

Maniac Monkey

Anyone running their own business will tell you that you will do almost anything to make it work, to be successful and to make money. I'm no different. I don't like failing, and for lots of reasons, some which weren't my fault, I have occasionally failed quite badly along the way. I opened a small street tour agency in Alanya, and bugger me, it was the same year a war started which freaked the foreign office out, which in turn freaked the tourists out. They stopped coming.

My little agency was only just holding its own. I was paying the bills and the wages of Fehmi, the guy who I had found to help me manage it, but I was taking very little money from it. I needed to up my game in some way shape or form. My business partner, Cevat, had a bus company. Some of his buses and drivers were working in Alanya, and they were sleeping in the shop. They always stayed out of the way if I had customers and were normally only there during the night. The shop had an upstairs where the office was. It was carpeted up there, so that's where they slept. They were quite comfortable compared with some of the alternatives they had. It was by choice, as they could have used the overnight allowance which Cevat gave them, but they always chose to send this extra money home to their families.

A few minutes' walk from where my shop was located, there was another tour shop. He had been there for years and was in a brilliant spot right on the main road, which in those days ran down the coast at the side of Cleopatra beach. That road has now been made into a pedestrian walkway and is now one-way.

This other shop was right on the junction, so he was busy before the road was altered due to it being the main road, and now he's busy because he has extra footfall past his shop.

He had what seemed like a really clever way to get people to stop. He had a small capuchin money sitting outside. During the day, the monkey would sit in, or under one of the trees that were growing along the side of the road. There was a long branch with a V at the top, and in the evenings the little fella would sit on that. He wore a little fez and the kids loved him. He was calm and friendly, and the kids loved to feed him the fruit, nuts and leaves given to them by the tour shop staff. Whilst the kids played with the monkey, their parents were able to sit in relative peace to discuss and buy trips. Win, win.

This little money was very clever. He could do tricks with a coin, and he really was very entertaining. I have a photograph somewhere, showing my older brother and I standing somewhere on holiday, possibly Great Yarmouth, and we were both holding one of these little capuchins. When I was older and saw the photo, I commented how cruel it was, how could people use these animals to make a living. It was unfair, they were probably kept in bad conditions etc etc. Yes, I was there with the no cruelty group. But I guess my mindset changed for the worse when I was asked by the owner of this other tour business if I also wanted to buy a monkey.

Now, my heart said no for all the reasons I have just stated. But my brain said well, maybe it would help my shop make some money. I found it easy to sell trips when I had people sitting with me, but sometimes their kids would fanny about so much that the parents were forced to leave without buying. Would a monkey help me? I asked if it was the monkey I saw regularly, and was told no, it was his brother. Was he calm and friendly like that one? Yes, I was told, he was. Why were they getting rid of it? I asked. The reason was that the shop he was supposed to work for hadn't done very well at the start of this season and it had closed down.

I spoke to Fehmi. What did he think? He thought it was a great idea, maybe it could help to bring people to the shop who walked past the end of the street as well. OK, so I went back to the seller. I'd asked around about him, Fehmi knew of him as well. Fehmi had worked on the tours for a few years. According to Fehmi, the guy selling the monkey didn't have the best reputation, so that worried me slightly. I told him I was interested but the price was too high. It was too high, but he said I could pick the monkey up and try him for a week, and then pay once I saw that he was able to attract new business and help me sell to parents while their kids were occupied.

That seemed like a deal. I didn't have anything to lose. I asked one of the drivers, Bekir, who was in the shop at the time, if he'd take me to pick the monkey up. He said yes but admitted he really didn't want to get near it because he was scared of them. I told him not to be daft, the monkey I had met was lovely and gentle and really funny. I'm sure it would all be OK. We set off in one of the minibuses to pick up the new addition to the team and pulled up outside the place where we were picking him up from. One of the lads from the shop came out carrying a large branch of wood with a pole fastened on the top for the monkey to sit on. The branch was fastened into a piece of metal to sit on the floor and it was quite heavy. Bekir the driver helped load it into the back of the bus. It had to go through the side door and be laid on the floor behind seats. I'm not really sure what I expected. Looking back, I really was stupid for doing this, but hey ho, I'll try anything, once! I think I expected the monkey to be in a large cage so we could move him, but nope, he came out on the arm of a guy wearing a long-sleeved top. This guy was holding a small link chain that was fastened to a dog collar around this little capuchin's neck. He was very still and holding onto the guys arm as they walked towards me.

I hadn't expected it to be so close and personal quite so quickly. I had bought fruit and nuts and thought I would be ready when he got back to our shop. But how could a normally fairly smart women be so off the bloody mark? The guy passed the chain to me, and it dawned on me that consequently the monkey was expected to travel sitting on my arm. I was still reasonably OK with that. Bekir, meanwhile, was bricking it. He just wasn't feeling it for this monkey at all. When it was all over, I did tell Bekir that I thought he was some kind of witch, because he had known in advance what was going to happen.

The little monkey reluctantly moved onto my arm. I tried to calm him, but what the feck do you say to a monkey? Come on, what? I climbed into the front seat of the minibus but stayed close to the door so that the monkey would not be sitting directly next to Bekir. Bekir climbed in, started the bus and we pulled away. This seemed to be some sort of signal for the monkey. I'm normally pretty good at describing places, situations and people, but the scene that followed is indescribable.

I'd suddenly got a little maniac on my arm. I knew now why long sleeves were needed. It was scratching me to pieces and would have bitten me if I had let it. But I was not having that!

As Bekir drove, I squealed. Bekir then squealed, so the monkey squealed. It was a scene from a horror movie. The bloody thing was trying to jump about but was on the short chain which was in my hand. Almost every time it tried to jump it would land on my knee, although not always on its feet. But sometimes it would end up swinging about! I was not only terrified for mine and Bekirs lives, but I was also worried about this little fella here. Poor thing must have been frightened to death. He had been so quiet with the other man who brought him out.

I also had no idea how Bekir was still driving. I figured he was just trying to cover the short distance back to our shop in the shortest possible time. But the few minutes' drive seemed to take several hours. We finally pulled up outside my shop, and Bekir was out of his seat quicker than I have ever seen a human being move before. Not only did he get out, but he also moved several metres away from the minibus as well. Ha, easy to know who your friends are when you're in a tight spot!

I opened my door, but I have no idea how I got out. There's no point lying about it. Me and my new friend just fell out. I had absolutely no idea what to do next. I had this little maniac jumping all over me by now! But Bekir finally manned up and had the sense to pull the big branch out of the bus. He was swearing quite badly. I was swearing really badly, and I've no doubts that the monkey probably was too, as he was making horrible noises. The branch was stood up, and I walked towards it. The bloody thing, which was swinging and jumping all over me, and really trying to bite me, jumped straight onto the branch. I clipped his chain onto a bracket that had clearly been put onto the branch for that purpose!

I stepped back. Bekir put his arm around my shoulders and asked me if I was OK. Did I need the hospital? Noooo! I was fine. So, he left me to go make a tea, which, together with lemon cologne, is the saviour of any situation in Turkey. I turned to watch him go, because I wasn't overly sure he was OK either. As he opened the shop glass door, I caught site of my reflection. No wonder he'd asked about the hospital. It looked like I'd been in a crash! My shirt was ripped and one of the short sleeves appeared to be hanging off. I had blood all over my arm where the devil beast had been sitting. I had spots of blood on my face, my shirt and the other arm had a splattering as well! I had short hair at that time, but it looked as if I had been dragged through a hawthorn hedge, pushed back again and the pulled through a second time for good measure! What the hell!

The monkey was sort of straightening himself up as well. He started preening himself like birds do. Fecking thing. I remember saying to it, 'If there's any blood on you mate, it's mine!' So clearly that's what you say to monkeys.

Bekir made me sit and drink a glass of tea, even though I don't like tea! But I did calm down. He drove me to my apartment so that I could get cleaned up and changed. We weren't worried about the monkey, no one was going to touch him! When I got back to the shop, I sat looking at this innocent looking little thing, wondering what the next step should be. As I did this Fehmi wandered down the road to the shop. He'd been on his break as we normally worked late hours to catch as many tourists going back to their hotels as we could. He smiled as he saw the monkey and when he got nearer, he started towards it. I told him that I wouldn't do that if I were him, as it was dangerous. He just laughed at me. He wasn't laughing a second later when it made a lunge towards him! He nearly fell backwards, and he swore! The monkey had launched itself off the pole at the top of his branch. He did this little swing thing and then he was back in his place. He had clearly done this move a lot, as he made it look seamless!

So now there were three of us sitting outside the shop, about two metres from this thing. We were all drinking tea and wondering what we should do. A few tourists walked past and said hello and made as if to visit our little devil. But we found ourselves warning them not to. Bloody hell! All I needed now was to have a lawsuit because the bloody thing had disfigured several tourists.

I think I could write an entire book about that little bastard! But, to cut a very long story short, that evening the rest of the drivers turned up. We all then sat drinking tea and discussing the monkey. Some had sympathy for it. I think I really did. Some just wanted me to shoot it there and then, outside the shop. Some thought we should just take it back. But on the whole, when the discussion had finished, the general consensus was that maybe it was just very frightened. Perhaps if we kept it for the night, and fed it, and didn't hurt it, that it might be OK in the morning. We also discussed the chance that it had been drugged or was beaten and had been really afraid of the guy who came out with it on his sleeve. We all agreed that was a strong possibility. The problem was, it had to go indoors for the night. Now which of these gallant men would help me, I wondered.

I was still wondering that when I unhooked it and looked it straight in the eye. I had long sleeves on now and had brought an old fleece with me that was my winter go-to that I'd never gone-to as it wasn't cold enough. The fleece stopped the thing being able to nip me and scratch me, but it still jumped all over the place. The drivers and Fehmi all scattered. Some were laughing, some were squealing but all were several metres away. I moved the monkey inside the shop, we had already moved in most of the chairs that went in there overnight. We had left one chair standing and some carpet had been put on the chair and on the floor underneath it. Food had been put in piles close enough to reach, and a plastic bowl of water was left there as well. I clipped the chain around the leg of a chair. The monkey was still going bonkers, but at least it was indoors now, and would hopefully settle for the night.

The guys all drifted off. Fehmi went home. Some of the guys were working overnight and the others went upstairs to sleep. Bekir locked the doors behind me as I headed home for a hot shower and a Valium. If only I had a Valium! pffff

The next morning, I was up bright and early. I hadn't told the boys about the monkey yet as I didn't want them to go near the pigging thing until we discovered if it had calmed down, so they were off to school. I walked around to the shop.

I instantly knew something was wrong, as once again there were several men sitting outside the shop. The chairs were normally lifted outside onto the very wide pavement in front of the shop, and that's where Fehmi or I sat to sell trips. This was the first time I'd seen the drivers move chairs, normally it was Fehmi or me doing it. I reached the shop with some trepidation. Well I lie, not some. I was absolutely full of trepidation. I reached the chairs and the drivers all started talking at the same time. Fehmi also arrived and was trying to listen to them all so that I could find out what was happening.

I looked inside the shop. There was just one chair in there now, with a small animal fastened to it. The said small animal was fast asleep on the piece of carpet, but the piece of carpet that had been left on the chair was nowhere to be seen. The water bowl had been tipped over; the fruit was scattered but some had disappeared. I spotted two grapes stuck onto the wall. There appeared to me monkey shit everywhere, and I mean everywhere. Shit on the walls, shit on the windows, shit on the maps we had hung. How could there be so much bloody shit?

I sat down and listened to the story unfold. Apparently, the monkey hadn't slept all night. The three drivers who were supposed to be sleeping upstairs had hardly slept at all either, as it was making noise all night. It was jumping up and down on the chair, then it threw the carpet placed on top of the chair across the room. Then it started throwing fruit and nuts. The drivers had stood it as long as they could, but in the early hours of the morning they got up. They put the lights on, used the toilet and started making some breakfast at the back of the shop. One of them went to open the door because the shop stank, and they assumed it was Monkey poo. Just as this driver pulled the doors open, he realised he had walked into an ambush. The monkey had been quiet when he came downstairs, but now it had just started throwing some of its own shit at him!

After that, it just stood on top of the chair launching shit at them all! As I type this I'm laughing at the situation, but at the time when I was stood listening to this, all I wanted was to take the damn monkey to a zoo, to live his life out and maybe meet someone who would throw shit at him. But the one thing I did know was that he was going back to whence he came.

As I was watching, the monkey woke. There appeared to be no further ammunition handy. Fehmi and I cleaned up the used ammo and the explosions of fruit on the walls. Monkey shit stinks. I have to say it stinks really bad, but Fehmi and I cleaned it all up. The only problem we had now was this little sniper bastard sitting looking malevolently at us.

I called the guy I'd bought the monkey off. I told him that, if he didn't organise someone to come and get it, I would be bringing it back to him together with a bag of shit, as he clearly knew what he was doing when he tried to sell it to me! His reply, 'Oh well, it was worth a try'. He had someone collect it within the hour. It was the guy who had worn the long sleeves the day before. He smiled at me, unhooked the monkey which jumped onto his arm without a noise, and they were off.

It took a while to get the smell out of the shop, we tried lots of things, but it eventually went. I threatened all the drivers that if they ever told Cevat what I'd done, I would then explain to him how not one of them had helped, except Bekir. That frightened them enough to remain quiet about my Maniac Monkey, and they were told never to mention it again, ever. Otherwise, I would just have never heard the last of it.

Just like Tommy Cooper

During my time living in Turkey, I travelled a lot with my partner Cevat. He not only owned his own bus company, but he owned acres and acres of orange groves, and I travelled with him trying to find new customers for his produce. It was an interesting time for me, I got to see places that I would never have imagined, see the inside of factories and packing plants which were extremely interesting. I'd be invited to meetings in all sorts of places with all sorts of people, and basically do lots of things that women, and especially foreign women, wouldn't normally get the opportunity to do in Turkey.

On this occasion we were travelling in and around Kadirli town which is on the Çukurova plain. I can't say I saw much of the town itself. We were visiting a friend of Cevat's who was a radish farmer. We arrived at his office, and after the brief Hello and introductions, we jumped back in the car. Cevat explained that his friend was picking a couple of people up, and we would follow him there and then follow him to a restaurant.

We also ended up with passengers in the car, and the chat was about why I was in Turkey and how I'd ended up where I was. It took a while to drive up to the restaurant. As we drove, we were travelling upwards until we eventually arrived outside a stunning looking building perched on a very high hillside. As was often the way when I travelled with Cevat, I didn't really know the plan, but I trusted him, and I never worried. On this occasion we met several other people outside the restaurant. More Hello's and introductions were made, and then we were all shown into the restaurant. We were shown to a big table positioned near the huge floor to ceiling windows, which made up three of the four walls of the room.

The table had beautiful, pristine white tablecloths, with equally beautiful tableware. It looked very impressive. Once we were all seated there were somewhere between ten and twelve men seated, all chatting. I was seated between Cevat and the guy who we had met originally, who was, and will forever be known as, the Radish man. I couldn't remember his name even then. I was close to the window, and the views were spectacular. As always, I was initially asked lots of questions which I tried to answer in my best Turkish, with help from Cevat who had developed an ear for my Turkish and my accent, and could understand things other people sometimes couldn't.

But after a while the conversation, as usual, would drift off to business. I would listen and pick up snippets and generally people watch. The people around this table were all business owners, radish growers. I initially thought that was an odd thing to be, but afterwards I realised that it was no different to be a crocus farmer or a sunflower farmer. Or an owner of orange groves. There was also a guy who owned a car dealership, another with a nightclub, and yet others who I hadn't fully figured out. One of the guys who was seated at the other end of the table was quite the comic. Throughout the mezes (Turkish starters) he was performing various tricks with napkins and coins. I was too far away to see them properly, but the guys at the other end of the table were in stitches.

I was introduced to a couple of foods that I hadn't eaten before at this restaurant. The first was the nicest meal of Humus I've ever eaten. Food in that part of Turkey was, and I guess still is, renowned for being hot and spicy. Bear in mind that this was the early part of the century and although Humus is now readily available in all supermarkets here, it wasn't back then. Indeed, I'd only eaten it once before when I was in Hatay. My starter arrived and it was humus which was in a shallow terracotta dish. On top was a layer of pastrami with a drizzle of olive oil on top of that. It was warm. It was also served with a small basket of warm hand made bread. It was fabulous and I did try to recreate it again whilst living in Turkey but it was never the same.

The second new food was Pandora fish, which was not a winner. I don't like bones and this fish had more than its fair share of bones, which for me was the spoiler. But as with all Turkish meals, there was a huge selection of salads and dips, bread, lavas bread, which is like a type of pitta bread, and plates of cheese with walnuts. It was a super spread and was enjoyed by everyone.

The joker at the end of the table was still making everyone laugh. Napkins, coins, drinking glasses and a breadbasket were all being used in his 'magical' tricks. Deserts aren't really eaten in Turkish restaurants, deserts are normally eaten at Cake shops, but this restaurant had a few deserts to choose from. I chose a milk pudding from a choice of milk pudding, baklava and Turkish ice cream. I found it odd that day, that every other person chose ice cream. Maybe they knew something I didn't know, either about the milk pudding or the ice cream.

The deserts were brought out and served, and for a few minutes the conversation stopped whilst we all got stuck in. All of a sudden there was a commotion at the far end of the table. The 'funny guy' who I sadly don't the name of, was slumped over, or rather into, his ice cream plate. Everyone was laughing at him, telling him to stop it now, calling him a kid and basically telling him to grow up. A couple of guys had screwed up their napkins and were throwing them at the clown, and someone had thrown a small piece of bread at his head, which struck him and bounced back onto the table.

He didn't move. We were all expecting him to raise his head and do something unexpected and funny, but he never did. The table started to grow quiet and the two guys nearest to the clown nudged him and were, I think, still waiting for him to do something to make them jump. But still nothing. We were all very quiet now, and one guy sitting next to him stood up and lifted the clown out of his plate. At this point Cevat told me not to watch, and I stared out of the window. But in the reflection of the glass I could see a couple of people including one from the restaurant checking the clown over. Someone was trying for a pulse, another couple of guys had started to lay him on the floor, and I think CPR was undertaken.

Everyone was shocked, and bless their hearts, one couple also seemed very concerned about my welfare, trying to make sure I wasn't watching. A private ambulance arrived after what seemed like a long time, but I'm sure it wasn't. Everyone, and I mean everyone, were wandering around and talking on their phones. I'd been escorted to part of the restaurant that had large sofas and was given a drink, but was pretty much left on my own for about 30 minutes. When Cevat reappeared, along with a couple of the other guys, they all looked visibly shocked, and I was really glad that Cevat had not been one of the guys throwing napkins and bread at the poor soul that had left in the ambulance, blue lights flashing and sirens blasting out.

We discovered a short while later, after we had dropped off our passengers and were in the radish farmer's home, that the poor guy had suffered a massive heart attack and had instantly died. It was both sad but funny at the same time for the guys, as they said there was no other way that he would have wanted to go. People laughing at him was something he'd been trying to do all of his life.

Cevat attended the funeral the following day and reported back that although it was sad, all the guys agreed that there was no other way that the funny man would have wanted to go. But he was only 52 no age to die. We never went back to that restaurant again, but Cevat did think he was funny telling everyone the story and saying that their deserts were to die for!

For anyone of a certain age, can you remember how Tommy Cooper died. He was on stage and he crumpled up and fell to his knees grasping the stage curtain behind him. People were in hysterics as this was the sort of foolishness his stage show contained. But he was actually having a heart attack on stage. He died because of it!

The Man Has a List, the Ladies Have No Clue

During my ten years living in Turkey, I did meet many interesting, some unusual, and some downright odd people. Some were tourists who thought it was OK to get drunk and say and do things that they could never have said and done in their own countries. These people are, and forever will be plebs, and I doubt very much that the flow of plebs will ever stop. To me, the pleb list of things to do is long, starting with drinking way too much and puking on the nicely arranged flower beds in the city. Drinking too much and puking everywhere, including on themselves. It includes fighting, and they normally fight like Huge Grant and Colin Firth in the Bridget Jones film. And the male plebs seem to think they can say whatever they like to women. But sometimes they bite off more than they can chew.

Jules, a friend of mine, once knocked a Scandinavian man on his ass following his insult to both her and I. He was in his late twenties and part of a group of plebs. We were sitting eating a jacket potato at about 3am, after we'd left the nightclub we had been in. Pleb-man thought it was OK to say whatever he wanted, which was an incredibly rude comment, too rude to state here. Jules stood up, raised her hand and it came down like Thor's hammer and knocked him backwards onto his ass. His friends were at first stunned and then they started laughing. The pleb? Well he started crying!

Female plebs think it's OK to walk around the bazaar or around busy markets with bikinis barely on. Why? Even if you were a fabulous size, with a stunning body and face and hair its not right, but it's normally overweight, loud mouthed, extremely unattractive women? It's wrong, people, on so many levels.

But as well as the plebs, there are many interesting people that I was lucky enough to meet. I met one man when I was sitting with Jules on another occasion, eating Jacket Potatoes in the early hours of the morning. He asked if he could sit with us as the café was full and we said of course he could. We naturally started chatting. I'm not sure how we moved to the subject, but he started telling us how he made a living. He was, for all intents and purposes, a male prostitute. He was very open about it all and explained that he had 'a string' of middle aged women from all over the world looking after him. We were enthralled, as he explained that, although he had now managed to buy his own apartment, he had at least four ladies sending him his 'rent' every month. We scoffed at this. He was a very attractive man, well groomed, beautiful white teeth, hands that didn't look like they had done a day's work in their life, and neatly trimmed nails. He had told us he was in his early thirties.

As we scoffed, he laughed and pulled out a little book from his pocket. It was the most organised thing we had ever seen. Each page had the name of a lady. Every detail: phone numbers, addresses, personal information about which flowers they liked, favourite restaurants, favourite foods. And other favourite things which would, or should, make you blush. There were lists of things they'd bought him over the years such as the names of watches, aftershaves, clothing, phones, and other items. He laughed when he showed us the names of three ladies who had all paid him for his new sofa! He was so organised, but he said he had to be, so that he didn't make any mistakes. He wanted to wear the correct watch, use the correct phone, wear the right clothing for each of his ladies. He did say though, that every now and again he would say something had broken, or he'd lost something, so that he could keep up with latest trends. In fact, he had really sold it. He also said that he liked his recent phone very much, and unbeknown to the various ladies who had bought phones for him, he had sold most of them. Instead of constantly using different phones, he could now just use the same one all the time!

He explained that he knew he couldn't keep doing this forever, which was why he had now bought his apartment. They continued to pay his rent for him, so now he was saving for a car and was raking in as much cash as he could. When each of his ladies visited, he never spent a penny, and if he organised it properly, he could have someone out visiting almost every week of the season. Some even came out in the winter months and stayed several weeks.

Jules and I had lived in Turkey for several years by then but had never seen anything so organised. We knew Turkish men who were married and whose Turkish wives were happy with them to take a foreign lady as a partner in the summer months so they could 'earn' money from them, but this guy was taking things to a complete new level. We bumped into him sometimes after that, but never spoke to him if he had a lady with him.

When we were speaking with him, I had this thing stuck in my head that I'd seen him somewhere before, but couldn't place him until a couple of days after the conversation. Then it struck me. When I'd been working as a Transfer rep a couple of years before, I'd been on car park duty with another rep and whilst we were waiting for the arrivals, we stood chatting in the car park. The public car park was at the back of the bus park at the airport, so if you were dropping someone off or picking someone up you needed to walk through the bus park in order to get to the terminal building.

We saw a guy with a lady who was crying, they were walking from the car park and he had his arm around her comforting her. They walked into the departure area, and we said how sad it was, and we wondered if it was a newly formed holiday romance or an ongoing relationship and how hard it is to have a relationship like that. A few minutes later we saw the guy now walking out of arrivals, as once you entered the departure lounge you couldn't get back out of the same way, you needed to walk along inside the terminal building and come out of arrivals. He walked back towards the car park. Sad.

But about ten minutes later as we were starting to get our customers arriving, and were showing them onto their transfer coaches, my friend shouted across to me. She indicated for me to look over towards the airport. There was the same guy, carrying a bunch of flowers, this time heading towards arrivals! We kept our eyes open in between working and yes, a few minutes later, he was walking back to the car park with another smiling woman carrying a bunch of flowers! At the time we laughed, saying that his timing was absolutely perfect as with only one two-hour drive to the airport and he'd dropped one off and collected another.

That guy was the man with the list.

This was taking it to the limit, but every Saturday evening when working for Sun World Ireland, we would collect customers from one big hotel in Mahmutlar, a resort a few miles outside Alanya. Every week, without exception, we would need to practically prise young girls from their Turkish loves. The girls would be heartbroken, saying they would phone and text and be back as soon as they could. The guys would make the right noises until the girls got on the buses. But the following week, the same guys would be there with their new loves. If you ever spoke to them, they would laugh and say that they never paid for anything, and why would they not take advantage of these girls. Well why not indeed, I don't have the answer to that!

On the other side though, I was once seated completing my paperwork after collecting Irish customers. It had been a very long shift and I was definitely flagging. I did my arrivals announcement and chat, walked up and down the coach making sure everyone was OK and we switched the lights off, it was a late transfer and the guests would normally sleep through most of the journey which was just over two hours.

Behind the driver on the bus there were two middle-aged ladies and they leaned across and were asking me all sorts of questions, all relating to me being in Turkey, how long had I been there, did I like it, was I married. Lots of questions. In return I asked them how many times they had done this trip as it was clear from their chatting that they had been before. They told me this was their sixth time. They were both married, quite happily, but they were there in Turkey for a 'shag', their word not mine. They explained that they came over, at least once, but sometimes twice, each season, and found a guy to spend the week with! They said their husbands knew, but I always wondered about that. I was intrigued and asked them how they got their 'fella' into the hotel! They said they didn't. They checked into the hotel when they arrived but the following day after they had been sun bathing they would 'pick up' a fella at one of the local bars and check into a cheaper local hotel and 'sleep' there for the week. They popped back to their package holiday hotel during the day to eat, use the facilities and the swimming pool, to shower and change clothes. They would then meet their fella in the evening and buy them dinner and pay for their drinks. They seemed to be clueless about the men, who they even were, anything!

They were so open about it, but I didn't judge, it really seemed to be no different to the man with the lists. More naive, less planned perhaps. But everyone getting what they wanted?

The End of Turkey For Now (Mostly) But Not The Adventures.

When I got to the end of my first book, I think I must have sounded as if my life was over when I moved back to the UK. But it really wasn't. I married a truly great fella, and we went off having the same sort of crazy adventures, and exploring together, until the world stopped in 2020.

So, I thought I would share with you readers a few episodes that happened, and interesting things I've seen in some of the other places I've been to around the world. I've kept them short though, as this Fat Bird does still have her heart in Turkey.

I've left one big adventure out. I'm planning my third book to be the stories and anecdotes of a fantastic road trip we had travelling around New Zealand. So please, even if you only like the Turkish stories, give it a try once it's out next year.

I thank you all for travelling with me, for laughing at my amazing life, and I hope to join you over a coffee again soon.

Back to my adventures again now, here we go!

Do You Need A Push?

I know I said that tales from Turkey were finished, but this little story is from one of the first trips I took with David. I wanted to show him where I'd lived, I wanted to show him all the things I'd talked about. He'd been to Turkey before, but only on business, so really only saw the inside of the airport, the inside of the hotel and the inside of the factory in Izmir.

We booked a flight to Antalya. I was excited. It felt as if I was going home. Even now, when I get off the plane in Turkey its like home. Never been sure why, but it is. We bought the visas, even though having a Kimlik (Turkish ID card) I didn't need one. I could have just stepped in the queue with the Turks, but I didn't want to be separated from David amongst the sometimes horrific queues at the immigration desks.

Now if you have ever booked a rental car with to be collected from Antalya airport, you may well feel some of my pain here. Once through immigration, we went downstairs to collect our baggage then through the final door into the arrivals area of the terminal. We had no idea where we should be headed. We had landed in the newer terminal and I knew that the car rental desks were in the older terminal. We had a wander round the desks that were in the new terminal, change offices, a couple of tour companies, but no car rentals. Then we saw a small poster pinned on the wall. For our company we had to call a telephone number. A bit odd, but OK, we called the number. They took our names and flight number, and told us to be outside in a few minutes. We followed instructions and I think we were looking for someone holding a sign with our names on, but nope, nothing. Then we saw a white Avis car pull up to the section of the road where people were dropped off for departures. We tentatively approached the car as there was only one man in it and he smiled and climbed out of the car. He came over and said he had come to collect us. Collect us? We just wanted a car! He explained that he would take us to the old terminal so we could sort out all the paperwork and get the car.

Again we followed instructions and got into the car. A short journey to the other terminal and he dumped us unceremoniously on the kerb and drove off. So far, Avis weren't getting any customer service awards. We lugged our bags into the terminal building, but of course we had to go through the departures door. It was fortunate I'd been a rep for a few years, and had used this terminal. So I knew my way around. We nipped through into departures, and started the long walk to reach the arrival part of the terminal, where all the businesses had little counters and shops. We finally found the Avis rental counter. There were two men sitting behind the desk and neither of them seemed in any particular rush to help us. We coughed and asked them what we did about getting a car. They looked up as if we were really disturbing them when they clearly weren't doing anything at all. Names were taken, passports copied, paperwork signed, and then we were shown outside, but not to a car, we were directed across to a large car park to a portacabin.

Off we went again. Once at the portacabin there was a man who had clearly undertaken customer services courses. He was a nice guy, and showed us to one of the dozens of cars, all the same model and all the same colour, white, parked in the car park. But then before he gave us the key he discovered he had some paperwork missing and poor David had to run back to the terminal to sort it out and bring it back. David is more used to just flashing his Avis card and driving licence and driving off. This was not the best start to our holiday, we had been in Turkey over an hour now and we were still in the bloody airport!

Finally, we were negotiating our way out of the airport and then on the road heading to Alanya which was a little over a two hour drive. Its fairly straightforward until you arrive in Alanya itself. David learned the hard way how Turkish roundabouts work. Which is basically that they are give-ways, but sometimes there are also traffic lights on the roundabout itself. At one roundabout, just as we left a place called Serik, David scared me to death. He shot over a roundabout where he thought we had the right of way. He did this weave thing, accompanied with three or four car horns tooting at us! He just said, 'I think I've got the hang of it now'. But by the time we had reached Alanya, he did have the knack!

We checked into the hotel, which was on the main street down near Cleopatra beach, and we were able to park right in front of the hotel. After that though, parking was a nightmare and we were constantly looking for legal parking. We visited a few places. We went to Dim Cay, and we had a drink sitting on a floating platform over the Dim river. We drove up to see the Dam now restraining the same river. We travelled up to Dim cave and found it lovely and cool to walk through the cave. We travelled to Side, parked up at the top of the town and walked down through the lovely town until we reached the harbour at the bottom, along the front of Side and to the Temple of Apollo. Side is a stunning place to wander around. Then we walked along the path on the coast back to the top of Side and to the Amphitheatre. We loved Side, and for me it brought back a lot of good happy memories. Now I had made even more happy memories with David.

Another day we drove up to the castle in Alanya, we were having a lot of fun. As we sat one evening we decided that the following day we would drive to Manavgat, which, like Side, was about an hour's drive away. We had planned to go on the day Manavgat held it's market. It is a massive market which engulfed most of the town centre. We planned to do some market shopping and then drive out of Manavgat to the nearby waterfalls.

That morning, we were up early. We had breakfast and we were away. The drive was nice, the weather was hot, and as we neared Manavgat we decided to park as soon as we got close to the centre, rather than get stuck in traffic due to the market being set up. But, as we turned onto the road heading to Manavgat, all we could see were roadworks. Roadworks everywhere, and I mean everywhere.

Now, this is the first time that the following tale has ever been told. Its rarely been spoken about even between David and myself. No friends, family or even the boys have heard about this. Stick with me.

We did manage to park up, but the market wasn't as much fun as it should have been thanks to the roads being all dug up. Stalls were widely spread out, and we were striding over ditches and roads that had been dug up. Lots of traffic cones everywhere, and general chaos. We cut short our shopping trip and decided to just head to the waterfall and relax there. We headed back to the car and set off in the general direction. I'd travelled to the falls many times, although it had been a long time since my last visit. But, I knew the direction we should be going in. Hands up I take partial responsibility for what was about to happen, but who would know?

We weren't enjoying this car ride. On every road there were holes, around every corner there were traffic cones and signs for diversions. Terrible signs which were hand-written for the most, badly spelt and almost most of them appeared to have been moved from the place they were supposedly written for. Oh my! But we were in the thick of it now, going back would be just as terrible as going forward. We seemed to be moving very slowly and we were both getting a little more than annoyed. David was driving and trying to get through the roadworks carefully. I was watching for the signs and detour notices, and was really hopeless for anything else. The detours were going all through back streets. But at one point we both relaxed slightly as the road seemed to widen, and the holes and traffic cones had disappeared. We saw a sign with detour and an arrow pointing left. We turned left and were heading up a steep hill. I recognised this road and said confidently that if we turned right at the top then we would be back on the main road to the waterfalls. The sun was shining brightly and was in our faces as we headed up the hill. But not for long. As we reached the crest of this hill, we literally ran out of road! We hadn't been going very fast, thankfully, and what happened next all started to go into slow motion. The front of the car was sticking up in the air, but again, not for long. We reached the tipping point, and we seemed to be balancing over the edge of a long drop. Then, very, very slowly the front of the car tilted downwards, way further than it should have. It was the weirdest feeling ever! We looked at each other and then came to a dead stop.

The road which should have been in front of us simply wasn't there. It was gone, and along with the road, the construction team had removed much of the earth from under where the road should have been. I do hope I'm painting the picture for you. Imagine the back wheels lifted about thirty centimetres off the road. The bottom of the car, the undertray, is balancing on the edge of what was effectively a cliff, of about a two metre drop. The front bumper of the car is touching a pile of rubble where the road should be. David and I were sitting in it. Now, my weird sense of humour wanted me to laugh, it wanted me to laugh so badly but when I looked at David, I thought better of it. He had gone a funny colour and just didn't look happy at all!

Somehow, we both managed to get out of the car and stand back so we could have a look. It wasn't good, it so wasn't good. We tried at first to weigh the back of the car down to see what would happen, but we discovered that the car wouldn't roll or move any further as there was a metal man-hole cover in front of it, sticking up and preventing the car from moving. We looked at the front. We checked everywhere, but really had no idea what the hell to do. By now we were gathering a little audience of men of varying ages. They all had an idea about what we should do, but none of them were feasible. We looked in the car and found the paperwork and on it there was a telephone number for emergencies. Before we called the number, I asked David to wait first.

I walked down the hill to the junction where we had turned into this fateful street. I watched the traffic going past until something larger than a car was coming along. I stepped out into the road and flagged him down. It was a nice young guy and he was in a pick-up. When I explained and pointed to our car and asked for help, he was willing to try. And bless him, he tried so hard. With David's help, they hooked up the car. We had already decided that the only way to move this car was backwards, pulling it off the 'cliff' back onto the road. The crowd of 'helpers' was getting bigger. We had now been joined by an older man who had lived in Germany, and spoke what seemed like really fluent German. He was speaking a lot of it! I told him, in Turkish, that we didn't understand him. Could he please speak Turkish? But he continued in German. We continued with setting up for the tow.

But the pick-up just wasn't heavy enough. All that happened was that the wheels of his truck would spin and spin. Our crowd of 'helpers' helped us pack stones under the front of the car in the hope that it would help. When it didn't, they all then gave up and walked off, telling us it was 'impossible'. Some were taking photos on their phones. David's colour was changing to red, and my sense of humour had decided it was not the time!

The young man with the pick-up who had by now been there about thirty minutes. He apologised, but said he would have to go. David gave him some money which he didn't want to take, but we told him it was to say 'thank you' and he took it and drove off. Then the old man switched from German to Turkish. He said he had a friend with a tractor. Would he like us to call his friend? Urrrgghh, yeah! All this time he'd been sitting chattering away in German, but at least now he said something useful in a language I could understand.

He called his friend and then said, his friend would come help us but wanted some money. It was a reasonably small amount and he was coming to us, so we said yes. We waited about thirty minutes for him. Meanwhile, we had a lot more people coming to 'help' and give their ideas, then walk off once they realised it wouldn't work. Everyone walking past was clearly an expert in dealing with cars hanging over cliffs. The most annoying thing of all was the number of people that told us there had been cones across the road, and a tape. But someone was constantly removing them, and putting the detour sign in the wrong places. Telling us that at this point was just not a help, it really didn't help.

When I look back at that day, I wasn't really that worried. In Turkey everyone knows someone who can help, there is a way of sorting everything, and as our little man on the tractor drove around the corner I knew this was our knight in shining armour. Well at least our knight in a scruffy green overall, but hey he was THE man!

He and David, watched by our German speaking Turkish friend, fastened some rope he had brought with him to the back of the car. Once it was secure, he jumped back onto the tractor, fired it up and pulled. Slowly, very slowly, our rental car started moving. I watched, hoping that it would be in one piece as it came back from the cliff edge. OK that is a little dramatic, but it effectively was a cliff to our little car. I hoped that the plastic under-pan was still in place, and that I wouldn't see oil, fuel or any other kind of fluid leaking out.

But no, a couple of stop and starts later our car was back with all four wheels on the road. No visible damage, but the underside must have been badly scratched. No fluids leaking or dripping anywhere. We unhooked the car from the tractor and David climbed in and started the car. Success! The tractor driver was paid, the German speaking man was given something as well, and we were back on the road in the car. We, very slowly, very carefully, negotiated our way through the roadworks and still went to the falls. We needed a drink.

For the rest of our holiday we constantly checked the car to see if anything was dripping or if anything appears broken. Fortunately, we were lucky and everything was OK. When it was time to take the car back to the airport, we discussed whether we should tell them, but decided there was no point, it was all underneath. For all we knew, it would be nothing more than a scratch.

When I started writing this book, I did think it was time to out this traumatic episode. Strangely, at the same time, David was thinking 'why not?'. So here it is.

David also said something funny a few months after this. He said that, at the time of the incident, he had no idea that things like this had been happening to me for years! Bloody cheek!

Paris

When most people write about Paris, they would tell you about the amazing sights, as it is undoubtedly a beautiful place. Fantastic places to visit, the sights, the smells, the food, yes that is all fabulous, but as this is my book, I thought I might do it slightly differently.

David and I were lucky enough to be heading for Paris on the Euro Star. I love this form of transport. I love trains and the ease of travelling on them. Down to Kings Cross, across the road to St Pancras and to the Euro Star check in. Onto the train and hey presto, off at Paris. Then you find yourselves singing Charles Aznavour songs far too loudly or talking like Jeanne Moreau. Or maybe that's just me as I have watched way too many old black and white films!

Anyhow, for my birthday a few years ago, we decided that Paris was the place to visit. My birthday is in February and we knew it would be cold, but we were prepared. David has his cold weather gear, which basically consists of a woolly hat and gloves. From all the places we have visited I can now boast a large collection of hats. Most of which I would only wear when I am abroad, where people don't know me.

Before we travel to any new places, I normally check out the Hop on Hop off bus tours, and Paris was no exception. I booked a two-day ticket, and these are great. On the first day we normally stay on all the way around, we listen to the commentary and David, who has a great sense of direction, mentally sorts a route for the things we want to explore further on our second day. On the second day we hop on and off the bus visiting those places. It works very well, and I would recommend these tours to anyone.

We arrived in Paris. I was so excited, I had turned into Charles Aznavour now, there was no stopping me as we walked from the train station to our hotel, following the sat nav it should have been an easy ten minute walk. We arrived at the magnificent Hilton Paris Opera Hotel (thanks to those points again), and I'm always amazed when the Hilton hotels let me in! Especially when, as today I was in good form and had just started my fourteenth rendition of 'She'. I also know that as you read this, many of you of a certain age will be humming or singing 'She'. It is an ear worm, but I'm not sorry in the least.

The entrance to the Hotel was spectacular, all marble, chandeliers, beautifully polished wood everywhere, and impeccably groomed, extremely polite staff. We were shown to our room, and our Paris adventure had truly started. That evening we went out for dinner. We love to find quirky, off the beaten track places, and this evening was no exception. We ended up at the bottom of a run of steps that, for a fat woman looking up at them, looked like the North Face of some mountain. One that, as yet no one had managed to conquer. We were at the bottom of several flights of stairs, on the Right Bank of Paris that led to Montmartre and the Sacre-Coeur Basilica. This is the highest hill in Paris, and we had found it! I was determined to reach the top without a heart attack or without showing myself up, so I took the stairs in small bites, taking every chance to turn and admire the view, whatever the view was, whilst catching my breath. Reaching the top was certainly worth it as it must be one of the most romantic parts of Paris, narrow cobbled streets, small shops, bars and bistros scattered around the huge Basilica. It was dark when we got to the top and the Basilica was lit up and the whole place was dream like. I half expected Van Gogh to wander round a corner with a glass of wine in one hand and his ear in the other!

Later that evening, we found a funky little bistro where almost every table was in a tiny room on its own. The building itself was totally wonky and had a lot of steps, corners and places that the poor waiters must have hated. But the service and the food were both really good and we left for the hotel, happy, satisfied and ready for more of Paris.

The following day was the first day on the bus, so after a breakfast of all the good things in life, we headed out onto the streets of Paris to find the bus stop for the tour. That proved to be more difficult than we expected but we eventually found it near the fabulous Opera House. The bus arrived and we swapped our online tickets to 'real' tickets. We were away.

Ear plugs in, language selected and we were instantly listening to my friend Charles, but this time he was singing 'Formidable', a song, which I have to say David got stuck with as an ear worm and he sang it for weeks afterwards. Well, he sang about nine words of it, but it was very sweet.

That day we saw the Place de la Concorde with is huge big wheel, we went past the Louvre and it's weird eyesore of a glass pyramid, but that's just my own personal opinion, but it really is the oddest thing dropped into the oddest place in my eyes. Still amazing, but nevertheless odd.

We travelled past museums and many other buildings with history attached and crowds surrounding them. The music then changed, and on came Joe Dessin and Champs-Elysees. Now, I typed that as if I knew who he was, but that was googled afterwards because we loved the fun of the song and the tour so much. Up the Champs Elysee we travelled, singing along with Joe. We heard from the commentary about the Arc De Triomphe, it's history and the stories of the traffic driving around it.

Onwards and we drove past the famous Notre Dame, on past the Latin Quarter, and joy of joys, we turned a corner and there we were on a bridge going over the Seine heading straight for the Eiffel Tower. Surely this structure is what Paris is all about?

We stayed on the bus, singing and admiring all the wonderful views until we had done the full circle and we climbed off, already planning which places we would visit the following day.

Now, stay with me, I am getting to the part I really want to share with you and what has, and will always stick foremost in my memory about Paris. Bear with me, almost there.

Just for clarification, a lot of my adult life, I have been followed around by war and terrorism of some kind, as you would know if you have read about my times in Turkey. So, I would like to state first of all, that the fire in Notre Dame, which happened very soon after our visit, was nothing to do with me. I just took pictures of the place.

Secondly as with all good memories or all good adventures and trips, it's not the ones you planned, or scheduled, or dreamt about that turn out to be the best. In most cases it's the unplanned, never to be repeated, unexpected ones which stick in your memory.

On our second day we used the tour bus as a taxi. We had wandered around the glass pyramid at the Louvre. We didn't join the queue to go in as it was like a queue for Tesco's during the lock-down, so we gave it a miss.

We jumped off the bus and wandered around Notre Dame, such an historic place, and such a shame it later caught fire.

From Notre Dame we crossed the road to the Latin Quarter, which was a pretty cool place, the former haunts of Hemingway, Picasso and Jean-Paul Sartre amongst others. This was the heart of the Paris book trade. Sadly, publishers have been largely replaced by the fashion business, but it still remains a smart and very attractive part of the city. We had a lovely cup of hot chocolate there, I do remember the important things too. And in this part of Paris, you'd think that, if we were shopping, we might have bought maybe a book, maybe some stylish piece of clothing? Naww. I bought a humungous bag of 'to die for' chocolate!

Back on the bus and on towards Eiffel's Tower. I was a bit disappointed as we discovered that you aren't allowed to even walk underneath it without joining another supermarket lock-down queue to buy a ticket. We decided to give this a miss, as there just isn't enough time in our lives to queue for everything. Instead we found a remarkably quiet road down the side of the tower, and walked along the fronts of some rather large apartments that must once have been the most spectacular places, but that were now sadly like poor relations that had been left to fend for themselves. Crumbling paintwork and crumbling history. But from this road we had an amazing close up look at the tower which was just a few metres away.

We had booked onto a boat trip which was included with our Bus Tour ticket, so across another road and down to the boat on the Seine. We had our first French Crepe, sitting at a River side café. Then, a ride on a ferry, which might have been fabulous had we not been joined by thousands of school kids. OK so maybe not that many, but a lot, and of course kids need to learn their history and know about things other than their phones and games. But they stopped our trip from being fabulous and moved it down to the merely very good category.

Now we are back on the bus and heading to the Champs Elysee. We really wanted to see this. We had planned to jump of the bus and do what lots of other tourists were doing, and stand in the middle of the road and take a selfie with the Arc de Triomphe in the background, and then possibly see, if it was possible without queuing three days, to climb to the top. We had seen people up there the previous day when we drove past.

Now, set the scene in your mind, we are on the top deck of the double decker tour bus, left hand side. We hadn't managed to get front seats, but we were on the seat behind, hoping that we could jump into the front seats for better photos if anyone moved. There is a middle aged couple sitting directly in front of us, and the front seats on the right hand side of the bus there is a huge American lady with a polyester 'fur' coat on and bright orange hair, and her partner.

We plugged our headphones in, and David was sitting in the aisle seat, so he had to lean across me to plug his headphones in, which he did. We settled back with Joe Dessin; you should look him up as the Champs Elysee song really set the stage for this part of my story.

I have a nice engagement ring, it's very pretty but it does sometimes, not often, but sometimes snag on clothes. Often, when I look at it, I see that I have fuzzy little fibres attached to it, and I'm not always sure where I hooked them up. Now, as I sat singing along with Joe, the bus pulled away from the Place de la Concorde, heading up the two kilometre Champs Elysee to the Place Charles de Gaulle with the wonderful Arc De Triomphe standing proudly on the brow of a slight incline in the road. Sounds lovely doesn't it? Romantic? What could spoil this image, this was my birthday, I was with a man I love more than life, in a fabulous place, the sun was shining, and life was good!

Ah but wait, when I plugged in, I sat back so David could reach across and sort his headphones out, then as he finished, the lady sat in front of me, did that thing that some women with long hair are always doing. You know, the way nits used to be spread when you were at school. They put both hands under their hair at the nape of their neck and they sort of flick their long hair up and back, so if you're sitting behind them you either get a face full if you're close enough or a desk full and the potential to catch nits if you're at school. I had my left hand on the handrail of the seat, this point is important to help set the scene.

At this point I realised, instantaneously, that this lady's hair was super tangled in my engagement ring, and that her hair wasn't hair, it was a hideously bad raven black wig! Describing this is really difficult, but can you remember when you were a kid, there was a certain type of nylon rope that was kind of twisted and was, in my memory, nearly always a bright blue colour. You could, for whatever reason unpick it and it was then fine wiggly nylon sting, and if like many of us did, you went through that stage in life where you like to set fire to things, if you ever set fire to it, it kind of crackled and just shrivelled away. Well this lady had a wig made of the same stuff. If you missed the blue rope stage in your life, just try and imagine a really bad Halloween witch wig and you are on the right track.

Anyway, I'm now sitting, trying very hard not to laugh as I have an engagement ring stuck in her wig and I'm really not sure if I should just pull, but that might risk pulling her wig off, should I sit and try and unpick the tangle or should I just borrow David's lighter and shrivel my way out? David looked at me and I indicated my dilemma. Now he could have been helpful here, he's an engineer, a practical man who is never out of ideas! But he started laughing, then I laughed more, and we caught the bug. The more we tried to stop, the worse it got. Thankfully the bus was moving very slowing through the traffic, but I really wasn't sure what to do.

As we neared the Arc De Triomphe, I could see that the couple in front were collecting themselves, clearly ready to get off the bus.

It was now or never, if I didn't do something, she would get up, with the good chance of leaving her wig on the seat, or with me having to follow behind her for the rest of the day. Ok so here goes, I use my right hand to hold the hair in front of me on the seat handle whilst at the same time I quickly tug my left hand out of the mess of nylon hair I was tangled up in.

Now imagine this, it all happened very quickly. Freeing my ring had worked, and even though David was laughing really hard at my predicament, he also planned to take advantage of the fact that the front seats would soon be empty and move onto them so he could get some good pictures before we then jumped off the bus at the next stop. As I was extracting myself from the black hair, David leaned across to take his headphones out of their socket, ready to jump into the front seat.

You still with me here?

At the very same moment the couple in front of us got up, the lady being a little lighter as I had a lot of her hair still with me, and David was leaning over to unplug his headphones, the incredibly huge American lady also jumped up. Even though she was already on a front seat. She clearly wanted four front seats between her and her partner and she seated herself on the seat in front of us. A second later she too did the hair flicky thing at the same time David raised his head, directly into a very orange wig! This one was equally as awful as the first, made from the same stuff, but this one was orange and black and formed into tiny, tiny ringlets. And David got a face full!

He doesn't swear in public very often, but his 'What the Fuck!' comment just pushed me over the edge.

Have you ever been to that place where you start to laugh, your friends laugh with you, sometimes they don't even know the reason, but no matter what you do, you can't stop? Well that's how I remember the Arc De Triomphe. We missed our stop, and I really can't remember where we did exactly get off the bus as we laughed until we cried. Maybe it was one of those things, that you had to be there. But I had an addition to my engagement ring that was like ewwww to take out, and David was spitting fake ginger pubic-looking hair out of his mouth!

Now tell me, in the same circumstances, what would you remember Paris for!

David Has His Bits Knocked Off!

A couple of years ago, David and I were lucky enough to fly off to Italy for another of our fabulous trips. This time we were pushing the boat out and the trip started with landing in Verona where we would pick up a rental car. The planned itinerary included a couple of nights in Florence and Venice, a few more in Lake Garda and a couple of nights in Verona itself, from where we would catch a flight back. Quite a hectic plan, but we could do it.

As always, I'd check out what to do, what to see, where to go when we were in all these wonderful places. There were lots!

Take Florence. This started off slightly stressful as we drove into Florence itself. We hadn't realised that the apartment we were staying in was so close to the actual centre of Florence. It was just a short walk from the Duomo, the large Cathedral of Santa Maria de Fiore, probably the things that pops up first if you search Florence on the internet. Parking and the one-way system were the issue. We both became frazzled and at one point I drove whilst David used his Sat Nav, but we decided it was impossible. We gave in and parked in the Train Station Car park, walked to the hotel, thinking David would return for the car once we'd checked in and arranged where the valet parking guy would meet him.

The place we were staying in was a strange one. It was basically a very large room of an equally large apartment and the owners had made this large room into a bedroom and bathroom and it was all done really well. So, each room in the apartment was a room to rent. We had a beautiful four poster bed with beautiful bed linen. A wonderful start to our Italian Trip. The receptionists explained to David the way to drive to the door of the hotel and she would organise someone from the local parking company to come collect it and park it up in one of the underground car parks. Worked a dream! If only we had known prior to arriving in Florence!

We headed out into Florence. We both love historic places and old buildings, and we were in for a treat. We came to the Duomo first, a building started in the 13th Century and one which is said to have started a whole new era of art and engineering. We started to walk around the building. It is truly a staggeringly wonderful sight, with statues and artwork and beautiful brickwork. We only managed to get so far round the back of the Duomo when we were stopped by temporary railings and big burly men holding everyone back. We had to wait a few minutes and then suddenly all the excitement was over. We discovered later that a movie was being made, and someone was being filmed up on the terracotta tile roof of the Duomo itself. We never did find out who it was, though. But the more recent history of Florence is littered with many films, some famous some not, which were filmed in and around the city and the Duomo in particular.

We complete our walk around the Duomo and decided to sit for a drink in the shadow of the bell tower part of this fantastic building in the Piazza del Duomo. We did, however, hope that it wouldn't be the same as sitting in St Marks square in Venice when it came to the bill. It wasn't. What a wonderful place, sitting with the sun shining and in the shadow of this amazing building drinking cappuccino with a wonderful man. Not bad for a fat bird who grew up in a coal mining village!

We were refreshed and ready to see more. First stop was to head to the Ponte Vecchio bridge which spans the river Arno. This bridge has shops all over it. In the past they were butchers and farmers, but the shops now are trendy jewellery shops and souvenir shops. Halfway over there is a break on both sides of the bridge, so a view of the river from both sides is possible and I'm pretty sure than in addition to ours, several million selfies have been taken there.

En-route to the bridge were countless museums, galleries, statues and wonderful points of interest within these historic walkways. But we were on a mission, so we took lots of photos but ploughed on to the bridge. We window shopped on the way across, took lots of photos, but once on the other side of the river we were aiming for the Boboli Gardens. These gardens were originally designed for the Medici banking family and a political dynasty.

Near the Boboli entrance we stopped for a cold drink then bought tickets and headed into the gardens. Once up near the top of the hill, the views looking back over Florence were well worth this fat bird puffing and panting her way to the top. The garden was dotted with structures and planting that was designed by the Medici family, but it became the forerunner for a lot of European royal gardens. It took us a few hours to walk the gardens and admire the view of Florence from the top of the hill.

That was our first day in Italy and boy, did we see history. We headed back to our apartment, stopping to eat on the way. Once in bed, I dreamed of how life was in Florence hundreds of years ago.

The following morning, we left our room and put our bags in the baggage room. We toddled off as directed by the receptionists to a local restaurant where we had breakfast. That had never happened to me before, and we laughed as we followed some other guests from our hotel in a line, just like a crocodile at school. We resisted holding hands though, and when we reached the restaurant, which was only 5 minutes away, we were greeted with a truly massive choice of food.

Today we wanted to visit the Medici house. This was also only a short walk across the road from the apartment we were staying in, so we headed back and paid for the ticket to get into the Medici house. The Medici weren't noblemen, but they were the richest family in the 15th Century. They were big pals with Leonardo DaVinci, and they commissioned many of his works of art, including the Sistine chapel and the statue of David, which is now an icon and the symbol of Florence. We wandered at our leisure around the Medici house, full of magical little rooms containing amazing tapestries, artwork and statues. There was hardly anyone else there besides us. We learned that the Medici had a secret corridor in Florence, called the Vasari corridor, which allowed the family to walk around Florence high above everyone in an enclosed walkway. Now how cool was that!

Before we headed back to claim our luggage and ask for the car back, we headed off to a small back street to find a fridge magnet. Yes, I do collect them every place we visit! We found some nice ceramic ones. They were mounted on a magnetic board outside the shop. I started looking at them and decided that one with the word David on it and the nether region of a man with a fairly large package was THE one for me. Well I had to, didn't I? So, I go to pick it off the board in order to take it inside to pay, but it jumped out of my hand! It must have, as I know I never dropped it. It all happened in slow motion and I heard the horrendous noise as it hit the pavement! When I picked it up, I had knocked David's penis off! Horror, but the man in the shop assured me it happened all the time and wouldn't let me pay for the broken David. I left Florence in shame! There was another David with no penis. At least the one I took away had a big one!

A Leaning Place

Once we left Florence, heading towards Venice, we realised that we were close to Pisa, too close to not have a quick visit at the leaning tower in all its glory.

We reset the Sat Nav and set off. Within an hour we were getting close, but the roads seemed to be tuning into poor roads. At one point we were driving through a housing estate with the strangest little bungalow type homes. Not at all the type of thing that we expected. I guess I expected something like Florence, or even the outskirts of Verona had been when we picked up the car. I expected it to be in a piazza with old buildings all around it, statues and ornamental columns and balconies. Have you ever imagined where the leaning Tower of Pisa is, or how splendid the surrounding area must be? Well don't bother. Trust me, you will never in a million years get the image right!

We arrived in what the Sat Nav said was the town centre of Pisa, although there was very little there to stand out. Nothing but a huge car park, and a handful of shops. Not shops as we had seen in Florence, but everyday shops. Little supermarkets, little cafés that belonged more on an industrial estate. We decided to have a drive around as we really thought we were in the wrong place. We spun around a roundabout and headed back the way we had come. Just before we hit the bungalow twilight zone, we turned right. On our right-hand side there was a very large wall and we travelled along the side of this for a couple of miles.

We were quickly in the countryside again. No tower out here, in fact nothing out here! We found somewhere appropriate and turned around once again. This time, as we travelled back into 'town', above the wall ahead of us I spotted the top of the bloody tower. So, we were in the right place! We headed back into the centre and pulled into the huge carpark we had seen earlier. We walked out of the car park and followed other people, they all seemed to be walking across the road and down the side of a large, but unassuming, row of red brick buildings. As we reached the end of these buildings, there were a few market stalls selling the usual mix of souvenirs of all shapes and colours. To our left we saw the big wall, and it was a big wall, like the wall of a castle.

We headed towards the wall. There was a huge wrought iron gateway. We once again followed the crowds and headed through the gate. In that single moment we were teleported back hundreds of years. We were back in the fourteenth Century. Ahead and to our left was a large and beautifully manicured stretch of grass. My gaze was then drawn to a magnificent cathedral, built from beautiful white marble, ornately decorated and such a surprise. In all the pictures I had ever seen of the tower, I can't remember ever seeing this cathedral. But it was staggering, absolutely staggering. As we walked along the pavement, we were both in awe of the sight before us. The tower itself is, of course, an amazing building. White and bright, and almost shining. Again, beautifully decorated with row after row of arches following the stairs around the tower. It was stunning, and it was indeed leaning. But when we looked closely, so was the cathedral.

The tower and cathedral were contained behind this huge wall, along with fourteenth century buildings that were houses and hotels. It was almost as if this wonderful site had been picked up and just dropped in the middle of an ordinary modern town!

The only annoying thing for us was the number of people. Men, women and kids all standing on a wall along side of the pavement. Everyone trying to get THAT photo. You know, the one where you are holding the tower up or pushing it back up. There were bloody hundreds of people doing the exact same thing. All along the wall. So, we did it too.

We reached the bottom of the tower and took a couple of photos. Next to the tower there was an army armoured car, which reminded everyone that they were in the twenty first Century and not the fourteenth. We turned and started to make out way slowly back to the gate, and out of this magical place. It was sad to walk back out into the most ordinary town in Italy. We sat for a coffee then made out way back to the car.

I would recommend everyone who has the chance to visit the Leaning Tower of Pisa. However, what I would also recommend is that, unless you are the one driving, you keep your eyes closed until you are through the magical gate!

A million Bridges

The next stop on our Italian adventure was Venice. I'd had a day trip there many, many years ago, when I'd been holidaying in what was then Yugoslavia. But a day is really nowhere near enough.

On this trip we had booked into a hotel which was on the mainland, one of the reasons being that we were pretty sure that we wouldn't be able to take the car into Venice. The hotel we booked into was on a main bus route, and the bus stop was at the bottom of the hotel driveway, so it was ideal. The hotel was another one we could pay for with points too! Well, I am from Yorkshire, after all. Each day, after breakfast, we would walk down to the bus stop, jump onto the council bus, and enjoy the incredibly scenic ride into Venice. The weird thing with our first trip though, was that we had to buy tickets after we got off!

Venice is a busy tourist trap, but we wanted to see more. In the two days that we had there, we did manage to see as much as anyone could. We visited the traditional must-see sights of the Grand Canal, St Mark's Square, the Basilica, the Campanile Bell Tower and the Doges Palace. Then we walked along the harbour side and saw the Bridge of Sighs. But David and I are like the advert about getting the most for your money, and we wanted to see more. Was there a 'normal' side of Venice were local people lived and carried out their lives, away from the constant hustle and bustle?

We walked and walked for miles. Down little alleyways, along big alleyways, around a million blind corners, including some corners that we thought maybe we shouldn't have been going around. We stepped out into some great places. Once, we stepped out into an area with lovely little houses on both sides, a garden in the middle and the Grand Canal at the bottom of the row of houses. But it was so quiet and peaceful. What a great place to live. We walked around several corners that led to dead ends, and so we would walk back the way we came. It felt like we were in the midst of a giant maze. Our favourite corner that we walked around was into a piazza. This piazza was not like the ones we had left behind earlier in the day, or the ones in Florence, full of tourists. This piazza had one small café in it. There were old people sitting on the benches of a small garden, there were kids, local kids, playing everywhere. There was no view or noise that would ever have let you believe you were in Venice. We sat at that café for a long time. It was such a wonderful, calming place to be.

After we left this piazza, we stumbled onto the Naval shipyards. These are former armouries and shipyards clustered together that dated back to the late Middle ages. Incredibly, in Venice, in the height of the tourist season, we had these shipyards practically to ourselves. Tourists clearly hadn't found them yet.

We walked back, going over the Rialto bridge. We also walked over the Bridge of Fists, a bridge with a weird history where the locals used to come between September and December in order to settle scores and basically have punch ups! That might not sound too bad, but think, this was winter, and the water was cold. The canal was also full of sewerage, so you would try very, very hard not to lose and be thrown in there!

All in all, Venice was a great place to spend wandering around for a couple of days. We ate dinner on the side of the Grand

Canal, we bought traditional masks for the corner of my hall at home that I keep all our souvenirs in, and we enjoyed the splendour and the history. And we walked and walked and climbed up and down over several thousand bloody bridges!

Armpits and High Places!

Before I tell my story, I need to remind you that I am no longer frightened of many things I used to fear, life has over the years toughened me up. Fear is a pointless thing in my view, and I have found in the past that the fear of doing something is normally worse than the doing. But I am frightened of heights, and I keep hoping that all the things I try that involve heights will help stop me being so scared, but not yet!

A couple of years back, David and I were holidaying in Alanya. I am very fortunate that he loves the place nearly as much as I do, so we try to have at least one holiday there a year. This particular visit included trying out the new cable car that travels from the station based just off Cleopatra beach up to the castle. Writing this however has brought back other terrifying cable car stories which I feel that I need to share.

The third stop of our Italian adventure was Lake Garda. David and I 'found' a cable car in a wonderful magical town called Malcesini, which is perched on the side of the lake. We had noticed this cable car when we were sitting on the first afternoon on our hotel balcony. We were having a quiet day and agreed that the following day we should investigate! 'Yeah of course we should' said I, hoping that the queue to buy tickets and use it would be three quarters of a mile long, and that we would have to regretfully call it a day and do something else, not as dangerous. We set off the next morning and David was on a mission. And bugger! When we finally found the cable car station, the queue wasn't long at all, so we joined the back of it and edged forward towards the platform where you climb into the car.

Now, at this point I need to zip quickly back to Turkey and explain about armpits and penis pushers! I know many ladies who read my first book have lived there or been visiting Turkey frequently and for a long time, so some of you may well have experienced this yourselves. But I'm in my time machine here and I'm going back to the late 80's. My first visit to Turkey was 1988, so thirty years, and things have changed. In those good old days, if you climbed onto a council bus, any of a number of things could happen, and sometimes they all happened at the same time. You needed to be brave and have a strong stomach on some of these journeys. It was, however, a great incentive to actually walk, and unless you were going a fair way, I would have recommended a walk. And I'm a fat bird, we don't, as a rule, chose walking.

Now imagine yourself, especially if you are travelling alone, sitting on a council bus all those years ago. During the season they invariably ran with 300 people on board, each shuffling and pushing to gain a safe place to sit, hang on, stand or lean on. It's this leaning and hanging thing where my story starts. In those days, men didn't tend to sit down next to a lone woman. Indeed, on my first visit to Izmir there were still buses running where men and women were actually segregated. But, in Alanya it was just not the done thing to sit next to a lone woman. As well as imagining you're sitting on the bus minding your own business, consider that deodorant of any kind was very, very, expensive to buy in Turkey. As a consequence, other than the foreigners, simply no-one could afford it. Have you got the picture in your mind?

You might be lucky enough to get a window seat and then another foreign lady sat down next to you. Then your journey was one of the better ones, top marks there. The next possibility was that you would sit down next to a foreign woman who had already nabbed the window seat. Mmm, not quite so lucky. The reason? Well, you might just have a group of Turkish guys who were hanging onto the straps in the aisle, and their armpits, complete with small dark patches on their clothing, were very, very, close to you. Boy, they did honk! But that wasn't the worst part. Some of these men took the opportunity to have some entertainment by leaning in very close and start rubbing their penises, or is it penisi, against you. Penises or penisi, they were rubbed against poor unsuspecting foreign ladies' arms. I saw it happen so many times, but never to a Turkish Lady. I suspect they would have ended up having their tiddlers snapped off as there was a possibility the lady's husband was close by. But foreigners seemed to be an easy target.

So, there you are, on a very hot, very crowded, bus. It's smelling a bit ripe, and now you have a middle-aged man rubbing his meat and veg onto you! After the shock of the first time, I became quite adept at elbowing said saddo in his nether regions without batting an eye. But some women were frightened to stand up to this, and put up with it until either their stop, or the penis pushers stop, came along. Being heavy as well, came in handy as a lot of the time these penis pushers had flip flops or sandals on so standing on them as you tried to leave the bus was always a good move as well.

Now that I've set the scene, return with me back to Lake Garda in Italy and the queue for the cable car. We climb aboard when we get to the front of the queue, and it always amazes me just how many people they can push into a small little fish bowl type pod, which will dangle several thousand feet up in the air. OK, so that's a slight exaggeration, but only a slight one. We moved to the front of the car, and are pushed towards the window, where at least I can hold onto the bar running around the inside of the cabin, instead of trying to hold onto the straps hanging from the roof, like the ones on a bus. I am by now terrified, but trying not to scream, cry or move. David is standing behind me with his arms around me holding onto the same bar. That makes me feel a little safer, but he can't stay like that as there are more and more people being squeezed on. He moves to stand at the side of me, and on my other side there is a very tall American gentleman, who was very polite and really very nice, because during this hellish journey he realised that he was standing next to a lady wimp, and he made random comments to make me feel better.

But, and this is where this story all ties in, behind me hanging onto one of the straps, was what I can only imagine was a Time traveller who had popped up for a visit from 1980 and was unable to buy any deodorant on his arrival to the 21st century. Either that, or he had something that had died a few days previously tucked under his armpits. Either way, he was one of the stinkiest people I have ever had the misfortune to stand next to. David saw me gipping and wondered what was wrong. So, I told him quiet loudly that something dead was in the cabin, maybe we should all evacuate until we found it! He didn't quite get what was in my head, which happens a lot with most people talking to me. So, then I told him clearly that I was standing next to someone who smelled really, really, badly. I had hoped that stinky would hear me and take his arm down and hold on somewhere else, but he didn't. The next time I looked at him, his girlfriend/wife had almost lost her head into his armpit furthest away from me. Her eyes weren't watering, she wasn't retching, she seemed generally non-plussed so I guessed she was also a 1980 time traveller.

The American, who was lucky enough in this situation to be very tall, was also getting a whiff. I could tell this because he had now turned from a nice, tanned colour to a greenish shade of grey. I saw him whisper to the lady beside him. He was clearly a lot more polite than I was. Several times, I loudly announced that I was feeling ill. The only good thing to come out of this was that I never really noticed that we had left the cable car station and were now heading upwards. I was concentrating on not being ill. I really mean it was an unwashed-for-several-weeks sort of smell. It had stopped me thinking of this dangerous feat we were undertaking. However, I wouldn't recommend anyone taking someone smelly with them to stop their fear of heights, it was a toss-up which was worse.

We arrived at the top, and I wanted to burst out of the pod and let the time traveller put his arms down, but we shuffled off in the reverse order to shuffling on, which meant that we were near the back. But at last we were off, and even the tall, polite American leant over to me and said a few words about stinky!

We headed off the platform and down the stairs. As we got outside, David was like a big kid and was running towards the side of the mountain we were precariously balanced on. I sat down outside, near a very high Perspex wall, and begged him not to go next to the edge. We were really a very, very, long way up on the side of a mountain, looking down a very long way to the lake. What was worrying me was that I had to get down.

It was, I have to say a staggeringly great place to be and I would recommend a visit to anyone who finds themselves in that neck of the woods.

When it was time to descend, we started queuing but as we shuffled forward I was surveying the crown around us to see if stinky was anywhere close enough to be in the same pod, but I never saw him again, so all I had to worry about on the way down was that the cable might snap. Well, it might!

After this adventure, we headed into the town and had a drink in one of the lovely harbour bars, we then bought a ticket to go across the lake by boat to a place called Limoni. It is known for lemons strangely enough, and I bought lots of things that were very smelly, but in a nice way. I covered myself in a fair bit of it as well. I was scared that stinky had rubbed off on me!

Since that day, David seems to like testing my pluck. We have been on cable cars in Madeira and in New Zealand. Now here we were standing in Alanya at the Cable Car station, waiting to do another one. This was one of the tricky ones, that doesn't actually stop at the top and bottom. You have to jump on and off while its moving! Not easy for fat birds to do this elegantly, but I'm pleased to say I haven't fallen down yet doing it. I haven't cried on the way up, or down, and I can almost look out of the window now! Oh, and none of the cables have snapped yet!

A Very Special, Special Place

As well as my adventures in Turkey, I really want to share a few adventures in my life after I left. I guess it's to prove that the fat bird continues to have an amazing life. My first book ended with me meeting and marrying David. Maybe it sounded like that was the end, but far from it. Before this horrible year changed all our lives, David and I were able to travel to some spectacular places. Many of which I never, in a million years, thought I would ever see or experience with such a wonderful travel partner.

The last stop in Italy was Verona. We'd had a wonderful time on the side of Lake Garda, and now we were heading for Verona. First let me explain, every time we go away, I try to help David with the costs as much as I can. Normally, I would buy something unusual, unforgettable or just pay for us to do something that will be a once-in-a-lifetime occurrence. So, I'd buy something like the two days of the big bus tours, or a helicopter ride, or a balloon ride. On this occasion, we had decided to split the hotels that we were staying in while we travelled around some of the most spectacular places in Italy.

Several years ago, I watched a film called 'Letters to Juliet'. If you have seen it, you will understand when I tell you that it's about Juliet's balcony. Romeo and Juliet were said to be based on real people from Verona. There is a museum which has THE balcony on it. This is a 14th century building. From it, you can see Juliet's house, and both places, especially the balcony, are massive tourist magnets. In the film girls pushed notes to

Juliet into spaces between the brickwork. If you haven't seen the film, give it a try.

When I was looking at the hotels we could stay in when we were in Verona, I stumbled on a great find. Let me set the picture here. The balcony of Juliet is set in a courtyard, and during the day hundreds, and I mean hundreds, of people would visit this courtyards to look up at the balcony and takes selfies, photos and sometime photographs of women who had stepped out onto the balcony whilst they were visiting the museum it is part of. In the courtyard there is a doorway to a shop selling Romeo and Juliet memorabilia. A shop that produced machine-made embroidery on demand, with names etc. There was a 'golden' statue of Juliet, one of her boobies now being silver as a result of thousands of sweaty hands rubbing and touching her. It is said to make you lucky in love if you touch her.

Nothing overly special, I hear you thinking, but all along one side of the courtyard, and both sides of the narrow entrance passage leading into the courtyard there are hundreds of notes, fastened to the walls. One section, which was on special boards is covered in graffiti. There was a post box on the wall. For what? Well to leave your note to Juliet. Where these letters actually go, however, are to a team of ladies who, between them, know lots of different languages. They are all different ages, and they are employed by Verona city council to answer these letters. Maybe one girl had fallen out with her lover, another was getting married and was suffering with nerves. Hundreds of letters in the post box waiting to be answered. The notes on the walls were slightly different in the fact that they were more notes to say they were sad, happy, in love. People's feelings were out in the open.

Between the hours of 9am and 7pm the gates to the courtyard are locked and no tourists are allowed in there. They would just stand outside, trying to peak through and to take photos. But in this same courtyard is the entrance to a hotel. This is one of the hotels I picked for our stay in Verona!

Now I've set the scene, back to our adventure. We travelled to Verona by car, and to make things easier, we had prearranged to return the rental as soon as we were there. I'd picked another hotel very close to the airport for our last night. We planned on taking a taxi to the hotel in Verona city once we had dropped the car off. We would then take another taxi to our second hotel back at the airport. Once we got back to Verona airport, instead of going straight to the car rental return location, we decided to have a quick check where the hotel for our last night was actually located. We followed our Sat Nav and pulled up at some closed gates which seemed to be the entrance into a strange flat roofed building which really did not look like a hotel. I was really worried, would one of the hotels I had picked, and in particular the one for our last night in Italy prove to be either a con or a dump! It wasn't overly expensive but come on, let's not spoil our holiday!

We had no choice, so we stuck to the plan, returned the car, picked up a taxi and headed into Verona itself. The taxi driver took us right into the city itself and dropped us outside a large gate. I knew what it was, but I hadn't shared this with David yet. We walked into the courtyard and there were hundreds of people squeezed in. We could see the balcony, but it was too crowded to see anything else. But, as we came through the passageway, we turned left. Two or three steps and the doorway of the hotel I had booked us into was right there before us. As we climbed the steps, a doorman appeared and opened the door for us. We signed in at reception and were shown up to our room. It was so exciting, the room and hotel in general was so luxurious. We were told that breakfast was served in our room, and we completed a menu selection and gave them the time we required it. There was a bowl of fruit in the room and the bedding was so splendid. I was in heaven!

We were told as we left the hotel that, when we wanted to get back in, if it was after 7pm, then there was a bell on the wall and the porter from the hotel would come and let us in. We wandered off into Verona. Like other places we had seen in Italy, the buildings were staggeringly beautiful. We walked down one narrow medieval street, turned the corner and found ourselves in an open space with a fantastic first century Roman amphitheatre. The weather at that moment was changing from a bright sunny day. Half of the sky was clear blue, and the other half was dark and foreboding. David took some stunning photos. One was a great photo of the amphitheatre in all its glory, with the raging sky behind it. But at that moment, we were standing in sunshine.

We wandered further and crossed the famous Ponte Di Castle Vecchio. Ponte means bridge and this bridge was unusual in the fact that it was built out of red brick, which made is stand out in Verona. We climbed stairs, not really my thing, but when sight-seeing I try my best not to faint, collapse, have a heart attack or generally show myself up. But we climbed a lot of stairs to get to the top of Castel San Pietro, The Castle of St Peter. At one time a church stood there, but in the 1300's a castle was built. It's not open to the public, but you are allowed to wander around the walls, and it gives THE best view looking back over the River Adige of Verona.

This place had so much to see and to offer that we just didn't have the time to give it justice. On the way back to our hotel, the rain had started. It was just that really annoying drizzle. Since we were almost back, we decided to stop somewhere to grab dinner. We stopped at a restaurant on the Piazza Delle Erbe and we chose to sit outside. It wasn't cold, even though the rain was continuing. All of the restaurants had outdoor seating with canopies of varying descriptions to make it possible.

We ate our meal and were sitting chatting when the strangest thing walked past. An elegant lady, wearing appropriate waterproof clothing clip clopped past us on the cobbles in the middle of the piazza. On a lead beside her, was a very, very large dog. We couldn't see it all, but we guessed it was something like a wolf hound. It was a seriously big dog, and its head looked like the shaggy sort of dog. But the reason why we couldn't say with 100% certainty what it was? Well, it had a tailored plastic rain mac on! The dog didn't like it, it looked at us and David and I were pretty sure it was asking us for help, it looked so embarrassed! A huge dog, not the normal dog to be seen wearing clothing, but this poor beast had THE flashiest yellow rain mac on. We laughed at the ridiculous sight, and I'm sure the dog looked even more embarrassed! One thing is for sure, David and I will never forget the poor thing.

We dashed back to the hotel, and as expected the gate was locked. There were a few people taking pics through the big wrought iron gate. We pushed the bell and seconds later the porter appeared with an umbrella over his head and another for us to shelter under. He opened the gate and asked the people taking photos not to enter, as David and I stepped self-consciously through into the courtyard. We thanked him and told him we would stay outside a few minutes longer, if we could borrow the umbrella. He replied that of course we could. He stepped through the door and closed it, and David and I explored the courtyard ALONE.

It was raining, which took a little of the shine off having the courtyard to ourselves, but we were able to wander around, read some of the notes posted onto the walls and passageway. We could read the boards giving information about the courtyard and the building. We took photos of the golden Juliet with the silver tit! All without dozens of people pushing and shoving us to move out of the way. Had it been dry I think we would have sat in the courtyard for a long time as it was such a calming place at this time of the evening, but we reluctantly went in and up to our room.

Another surprise, the bed had been turned down and mints left on the pillows. We had seen this many times on our adventures, but something I've never seen before or since had been done, a lovely piece of fabric with the hotel logo on was left at each side of the bed on the floor, so that, as we removed the slippers that had also been left out for us, we didn't have to stand on the floor before climbing into bed. Instead, we stood on the fabric!

The next morning, our breakfast turned up exactly as requested. It was served on a large table in our room. It wasn't cheap, but I don't regret a penny spent on that hotel room. I'm a coal miner's daughter from Yorkshire, I didn't do this. Historically I stayed in self-catering when the kids were small, or a nice but simple hotel, and this was all before we went to live in Turkey. If the boys and I travelled when we lived in Turkey, I was always on the lookout for a good, but economical hotel. Now and look at me! It was stunning, the view from the balcony looked down onto the piazza we had been in the previous evening. The room, the bathroom, the service, the breakfast, the courtyard. Everything was so fantastic!

I did imagine having this luxury every time I stayed in a hotel. But you know, I doubt that people who do that actually realise how lucky they are, and just how fabulous this hotel is. I'd hate to think I'd ever take it for granted. So, like we did, using it once is the way to go!

So, to cap off our stay in this one-of-a-kind hotel, remember I'm a Yorkshire girl, I packed away that little piece of fabric that was at the side of my bed. I'm not sure what I planned to do with it, but I still have it. I packed away all the slippers, which I do every time we stay in hotels with slippers, but I use them at home in the summer. I also stole one of the umbrellas from the umbrella stand in the foyer! Well I didn't actually steal it, I exchanged it for a clear plastic shonky umbrella that we had bought as we were wandering around. So, I swapped it! But karma is a bitch here, and I'll explain why shortly!

We asked if we could leave our luggage for a few hours and we headed off to explore some more of this city, which to be honest I didn't really know much about prior to booking our trip. Everyone has heard of Rome, or Venice and even Florence, but this place is worth a long weekend for sure. We found something around every corner, a new piazza where a there was covered seating to grab a drink or a snack, some had little markets in the middle, and of course it would have been rude not to do some shopping. And I'm not rude!

We revisited a strange little café/bar on the side of the river, where we sat outside on what can only be described as a large balcony, with dozens of other people also squashed into this small place. It had a great view, so it was worth the push.

We even found Romeos house, but it wasn't as busy as the courtyard we had left behind earlier that day. We reluctantly walked back to the hotel and managed to push through the tourists visiting the balcony. Once we got to the hotel door, we were given our luggage, a taxi was called, and we left probably the nicest hotel I have ever stayed in behind us. But I'd done it. Another memory to be filed away in the happy drawer!

Now the final stage of this trip was looming. Two days prior, we had called to have a peek at the hotel we were staying in for the night near the airport and it had been closed. We were a little concerned, but we gave the driver the address and set off. Even as we were leaving Verona, we were still seeing some fabulous sights and buildings. We reached the hotel in question, and the driver pulled up to the gate we had stopped outside on our visit. This time it was wide open, but it still looked very unlikely that there was a hotel in this building. We got out but asked the taxi to just wait a minute until we made sure it was a hotel and that we could get in.

We walked across to the only door we could find. There were no signs, no names, nothing. But the door was open and once we got in it was like a tardis, far bigger than we had expected.

We saw what looked like a reception desk, we quickly said the name of the hotel and they nodded and welcomed us in. David paid and let the taxi go. We checked in. This little place was really funky, it seemed newly painted and furnished so maybe it hadn't been open for very long. It was odd, though, in the fact that everything seemed to have a Mexican theme! This was in Italy, near one of the most historic cities, and this place was Mexican! We were shown up a winding staircase to our room and another shocker! A fabulous little room, again with a Mexican theme. I was relieved now, since this was another of the hotels I'd chosen and paid for and it was cheap, but the location for the airport was great.

We were told that the ground floor was a restaurant and breakfast was also served downstairs in the morning, but in a different part of the building. This building was massive and a real surprise. We tried to get organised and unpacked clothing we would be travelling in the following day, took out clothing for the evening, had a shower and packed the clothing we had been wearing. Now this is where Karma took a bite of my fat ass. I tried to get my stolen, sorry my swapped umbrella, into the case but it was too long! David laughed and said something along the lines of it serving me right that I would have to leave it. Leave it! Never! It was going home with the fabric, the slippers and us. In the end David found a way to remove the handle off so that we could fit it into the case. Bless him, when we got back to the UK one of his first missions was to glue the handle back on. The umbrella is in the boot of my car and is used mainly going in and out of work, it's a blue umbrella with the name of the hotel on it in Italian, and no one has a clue, no one cares where it's from, but I know!

Anyhow back to little Mexico We went downstairs for dinner and thought we might as well try the restaurant on the ground floor. There seemed to be little sign of other things outside the hotel. We booked a taxi to the airport for the morning and were shown into the restaurant. It was enormous, and clearly Mexican, which pleased David no end as he loves Mexican food. We were shown to a table at the bottom of the room which took at least three quarters of an hour to reach. OK slight exaggeration but imagine the biggest school hall in a UK comprehensive school, and that was the size of the room! The waitresses were all fast, attentive and very polite. We ordered our meals, and the starters arrived in seconds. An air crew arrived and joined us in the room and for a few minutes it was just us and them. This was a Sunday evening and we really didn't expect a place that size to get really busy. But by the time we had eaten our starters and looked up, the place was buzzing, almost half the tables were now full, and people were still walking in.

We were served with our main course after just a few minutes and were stunned once again to see the room was now completely full and we could see through the window that there were people queuing up outside. The meal proved to be a winner, which explained the restaurant's popularity. The place was a great accidental find, and David and I sometimes remember that night and that killer restaurant. We had stayed at two hotels in Verona, at different ends of the spectrum, they were both so memorable for different reasons, but all good. Someone said about my first book that it's not a good idea to judge a book by its cover. That's true for hotels too.

We finished out meal and went outside before we went to our room. There were dozens of people happily queuing to get in. We went upstairs, slept like the dead, and the following morning after a lovely breakfast we sadly headed to the airport. It had been such a wonderful trip!

Self-indulgent. You bet!

Whatever Next?

This is a little story, for which I have been given permission to put on paper. It involves my husband David, a man I love dearly, a super smart guy who is kind, generous and funny, my soul mate, my lover and my best friend, but…. David also has in the past done some very strange, unaccountable things when we are away from home and staying in hotels.

I've never really understood this, because David has spent close to half of the nights of his entire life in hotel rooms. He has travelled the world for his work, and he must have stayed in hundreds, if not thousands of hotels. Maybe it's just when he's with me? Maybe he does it all the time… who knows?

The first time I experienced one of David's 'turns' we were in Spain. We had had a lovely couple of days in Barcelona, we had wandered around the city, we had sampled Tapas, we had sat at a café on La Ramblas, a famous walkway through the city, full of restaurants and shops. We had eaten the nicest calamari ever eaten, it was thin and crispy and wonderfully tasty. We had drunk a substantial amount of Sangria and stayed in a hotel which was opposite a Gaudi decorated building which we could view from the hotel roof terrace. Gaudi designed the staggeringly unusual cathedral in Barcelona, and around the city there are buildings he designed, wonderfully colourful, which attract a lot of tourists.

We had then hired a car, and we drove down the coast to Cambrils, a lovely little place on the coast. This was the first time David and I had been on holiday together. We were having a lot of fun finding out about each other, and we laughed, we laughed a lot.

I need you to imagine the room we had. The head of the double bed was against one wall. On one side, the right-hand side as you look at the bed, there was a metre-wide space, then the wall with a window. On the left-hand side there was a metre gap, then a wardrobe, the back of the wardrobe being the bathroom wall. At the bottom of the bed there was a narrow gap and then an open shelved unit with a TV, but from the bed you could see the back of the TV. This unit was used to divide the bed area from an area where there were easy chairs for sitting to watch the TV. On David's side there was a gap for us both to get through to the bed but on my side, there was only a tiny gap as the unit was next to a sideboard type piece of furniture. There were curtains in this area which covered almost all of the wall. Picture set.

One particular evening, we had been out for dinner, we had eaten well and David had been drinking beer, then red wine, and then we had a cocktail on the way back to the hotel, but he didn't seem particularly drunk. We got into bed and went to sleep. I'm not sure when I was woken by David, but he was standing at the side of the bed. I'd turned the light on, thinking it was some kind of emergency. He was standing with his arms outstretched as if he was measuring something. He walked along the bottom of the bed, and how he did it I'm not sure, but he walked through the very small gap into the sitting area. How he never pushed the TV shelving unit over remains a mystery. He walked around the unit and back towards the bed via the 'proper' gap. Then he said loudly, 'I can't get out! I can't get out!' I was shocked but amused, and I realised he was doing some kind of weird sleep walking thing. He was trying to get into the bathroom and for whatever reason thought he couldn't. I directed him towards the bathroom, and he was off like a flash.

As he went into the bathroom, I walked into the sitting room area to get a drink out of the fridge. David came out of the bathroom and headed for the curtains, he pulled one curtain, then he pulled another, this created a gap with no curtains closed and he started chuntering on about the 'bastards across the road' watching him, and that the curtains weren't 'fucking big enough'. 'And not only that, but there was also a massive hole in the curtain!' I couldn't help but laugh and I directed him back to bed and he seemed to be off to sleep before I could go close the curtains. The next day, of course I took the micky out of him and we both laughed at his antics. The rest of the week was fine, no weird night times, so I thought it was a random one off. Ha!

Another of our trips was to Amsterdam. We had gone across on the Eurostar again for a long weekend on my birthday. We used some accumulated points and were staying in the Hilton. It is a tall building, and we were on the eleventh floor. We had a great view of the harbour area, and floor to ceiling windows.

We spent long days seeing the sites, wandering around shops and the saucy spots too. It was snowing lightly, and it was very romantic. We shopped and explored and were loving every moment together. One evening, as it was snowing heavily, we decided to eat in the hotel restaurant. It was a pleasant evening; good meal and we were sitting near a huge window, so the view of Amsterdam was great. David was drinking wine and had found a nice Merlot that he was enjoying.

We went up to bed, this time a fairly normal room with a large bed. Just one room with the bathroom near the door to the room. A standard layout which David must have seen hundreds of times. We went to bed, and at some point during the night, I heard David getting up to visit the bathroom, I assumed. But I sensed that he was heading in the wrong direction. What was he doing now? I sat up and waited a minute until my eyes had adapted to the room light. I couldn't see David anywhere. I knew he hadn't walked past the bottom of the bed so how had he disappeared? Then I twigged where he was. He was standing behind the curtain, between the curtain and a full-length window! I asked 'David, what are you doing?' and he did that thing that kids do when you've discovered them doing something that they shouldn't be doing. He spun around really quickly and said, and he said it way too fast, 'Nothing!' 'Then come away from the window', we were after all eleven floors up and thought I should move him away from the window.

He trotted off to the bathroom and I waited until he was out and back in bed before I relaxed again. The next morning, I asked him why he'd been licking the windows, but he couldn't remember what he had done or why! Weird David, weird.

This is last incident I want to share with you, although there are many more. I'm not sure why he does these things, maybe it's just that he has stayed in so many hotel rooms over the years that he is truly disorientated when he wakes up during the night, maybe the alcohol is an added problem, but whatever causes it, it can be incredibly funny.

We were on one of our annual road trips, it was the first in fact. We'd bought a new car and it was a convertible and was great fun to be in when the sun was shining. Our plan for this road trip was first York, then across the moors, stopping at Goathland where Heartbeat was filmed, then on to Whitby, which is one of my favourite places in the world and always will be, full of memories of wonderful childhood holidays. David had never been, so I wanted to share this wonderful place with him.

We reached York, and we had to park the car in a car park across the road from the hotel, which freaked David out a little, it being so new, but we checked in and headed straight out to explore York. The Shambles, the Minster, little markets that were scattered about, Museums, and the wall. A staggering amount of history. We even sat on the funny little buggies and had a ride through the Yorvik Museum which is all about the Vikings who lived in York. We ate, we drank, we sampled ice cream, we people watched, we shopped, well, I shopped, and we had a lovely time before heading back to the hotel. We wandered over to the Car Park and checked the car was OK, then we had a nightcap in the hotel bar and headed to bed.

The end of a lovely day you might think, but David still had one surprise in him! During the night at some point, I heard David get out of bed and head towards the bathroom. It really was pitch black in the room and I could hear him struggling and bumping into things en-route. As he came back out of the bathroom, I decided to help, so I turned my phone on so that the light from the screen could help him get back to the bed. As I did this, he had reached the bottom of the bed and was now perched on the edge of the bed, the light on my phone went off.

I touched the phone again to put the light back on, and just as I did so, I saw legs and a bum flash past me! Then I heard a horrible thud and realised that David had just done a complete back flip and he had landed on his back, headfirst on the floor at the side of the bed! What the fuck was he doing now? I lent over the bed to see David laying there rubbing his head. I had been worried, but now I realised that he'd landed on his head, I knew he'd be OK. That head has experienced bumps a lot worse.

Now my worry had gone the laughter started. To make it worse, David said 'Why do they have to make hotels with concrete floors?' I was laughing even more as he went on to say, 'I'll tell you how I know it's concrete'. I was now crying with laughter, he didn't stop and went on to say, 'cos I've just hit the fucking thing doing twenty five miles per hour'. Now, to this day I have never quite managed to figure out what he was doing, he doesn't know what he was doing. My only answer was that he was planning to just jump backwards onto the bed, but as he was sitting at an angle of the corner of the bed, he missed the bed!

Now these little stories are out in the open on paper. David will shortly be editing these words, so maybe they will never get as far as between the cover of book number two?

No Pigs, But What a Place!

Just after Christmas, as new year was approaching, David and I were sitting at home talking about holidays and we were planning which weeks I should book off from work the following year. We had to work around David's schedule, and he was very busy then. We had discussed the road trip, and where else we would go. This time we had planned to go to the Lake District for the road trip. We had even looked at the Christmas markets. We had just come back from Brussels Christmas Market which had been great, and we were thinking about Munich for the following year. We hadn't thought of the 'big' holiday yet.

I'd gone into the kitchen to make us a drink and as I walked back into the room where David was sitting, he said quite randomly 'What do you think about the Bahamas?' What did I think about the Bahamas? Well I'd never thought anything of the Bahamas, they were well off my 'places to go' list, I wasn't even 100% sure that I even knew where they were! David laughed when he saw my face and we sat together looking at the Bahamas on his laptop. I pretty quickly learned that the Bahamas were in the Caribbean, a long-haul flight of about nine or ten hours, but certainly do-able. That year David had worked a lot in the States and had accrued a lot of Hilton Honour points so we were actually sitting looking at the Hilton in Nassau in the Bahamas! Wowser! Within an hour, the hotel was booked for ten nights, BA flights were booked from Heathrow and I was sitting in shock that I was actually going to the Caribbean!

A couple of months later, we were on the plane. We shuffled into our seats and I managed to hear that satisfying click. No-one but a fat person will understand that struggle to get the seat belt around you quickly, remain comfortable and try to leave the seatbelt showing so that the cabin crew don't pick on the fatty to check their belt is secure, or even worse to offer you an extension!!!! But I was in, I was secure, and I was feeling good and happy. The flight went off without any issues, David who travels around the world and is used to flying, started off reading his book but he can quickly nod off. He wakes up whenever the trolleys come around with food and drink, then he's off to sleep again. I, on the other hand, find it difficult to sleep when I'm travelling, but I found a game on the aircraft media system and so spent a few hours testing my intelligence.

Finally, we arrived in Nassau We entered the terminal building and were ushered to the passport control area. An oil drum band were playing. What a wonderful way to be welcomed into a country. Once we had claimed our baggage we headed outside and looked for our name on a sign for transfer. We found it and were taken to the car for our short journey to the hotel. The driver turned out to be nuts, and as he was driving would regularly turn around to talk to us whilst he was driving. But we arrived safely, and the hotel was quite something. We had seen photos of course, but they didn't do this hotel justice.

We went into reception. We were a little shocked to see at least fifteen BA crew in front of us. This was clearly their stop over hotel, but David really didn't see that we should have to wait behind them, so he pushed forward and as a Hilton Honours Gold member the receptionist dealt with us quickly. We were led to our room, which was on the ground floor and had a view of the garden and ultimately the sea. We didn't waste any time and were quickly outside checking the hotel out. It had a seating area outside the bar and there were gas fire pits and easy chairs. Further down there was a gym, and a swimming pool with loungers and round sofas with canopies, an outside bar for snacks and drinks and then a beach. We sat in the bar and from there we could see in the distance four or five cruise liners. They were massive. And we soon discovered that at about 6pm they all left, and about 10 am the following day another set would appear.

That evening, we ate in the hotel restaurant and then wandered around to sit in the easy chairs with the fire pits, it was lovely, set in the gardens with tall palm trees swaying about and the sound of the sea. But something grabbed our attention. A couple of metres along from us there were two women sitting chatting. Loudly. We recognised one of them as crew from our flight, on their table there were at least a couple of dozen of the little wine bottles that you get served on board the flight! During the conversation, which we shamelessly listened to, the woman we didn't know turned out to be the girlfriend of the pilot, and had come over for a holiday. The cabin crew lady asked if she wanted to go for a walk into town, but then went on to say that when they got back, they wouldn't have to pay for any drinks as she had dozens of these little bottles in her room! Some paying passenger on the flight home wouldn't be getting her Prosecco, that was for sure. We were incensed and David, who didn't really rate BA anyway as he's had problems in the past with them, did find a few expletives that I'd never heard him say before.

On the subject of that BA crew, I'd like to add one more anecdote. One which I truly wish I had been able to record, as it would have certainly gone viral. We spent most of the time exploring the wonderful island, but one day we decided to have a pool day. We had settled into one of the tented sun loungers, both reading our books. Immediately behind us was a small hedge and on the other side of that, the beach. As we sat reading, I was picking up on a conversation on the other side of the hedge, I recognised one of the voices to be the voice of the campest male member of our cabin crew from the flight over. They got to have as much holiday as paying customers! His voice and manner were very unique. There were several other voices, and I just assumed they were the other cabin crew. There followed a conversation which left my jaw open in absolute shock. The camp guy was explaining to the other people how to NOT do your job! How to get around people pressing their buzzers, how to get around people requesting drinks and food items, and basically how to skive for the entire flight! I nudged David and he heard a little of the conversation. That was the moment in time we lost any respect for BA cabin crews.

Anyhow, I have seriously digressed again, Nassau was a nice place, not what we expected, but we met some wonderful people. Before we had arrived, I had checked out things to do and places to go. I had discovered that one of the things to do was swimming with pigs. Yes pigs. Pigs that lived free and basically lived to swim! That had been put on our list, and for me was at the top. During one of our early days there we had been looking around the Straw Market, a market which was packed, absolutely packed with clothing, souvenirs, bags, hats and handmade wooden ornaments. As we came out of the market, we saw a man across the street who seemed to be selling trips. So off we went, and he introduced himself as 'The Captain'. He was indeed selling boat trips of all kinds but unfortunately when we enquired about the swimming pigs, we discovered that they lived on a small island which was several hours' boat ride away, dinner on the trip was included but it was £400 each! Sadly, we decided to give the swimming pigs a miss.

During that holiday we walked miles, one day we decided to walk across the bridge to the huge Hotel and Casino complex on the other side. Another day e found a cigar factory and had a tour watching them being rolled. One day we walked to a lovely place that one of the young ladies that worked in our favourite pub had told us above called the Queen's Staircase. A set of sixty-five steps, carved out of solid limestone by six hundred slaves in 1793. It was an escape route from the fort, which was at the top. It was a really nice place and we visited it twice, the view from the fort at the top was well worth the trip as it covered the whole of Nassau.

The only issue we had with Nassau was that it seems to be set up for and revolve around the cruise ships. On the evenings, when we were sitting on the balcony of our favourite pub, we could see all the guests from the cruise liners heading back to their boats. Massive queues and sometimes it seemed to take an hour to get back on board, then shortly after that they were away, leaving the quayside empty for the night. But once they had all left Nassau, Nassau seemed to close! I don't just mean the shops, but the bars and restaurants. And the bars which stayed open stopped serving food. We hadn't booked all-inclusive, or even half board at the hotel, as we do like to sample the real place, but this time we were struggling. There was a McDonalds across the road, but we don't like fast food. We were advised to visit a place called the Fish Fry, where there was a large collection of restaurants. It was about a mile out of the town but a nice walk along the beach fronts, and when we arrived it was difficult to choose which one to visit, there were dozens of restaurants, all packed closely together.

We choose one and sat down, ordered drinks and were given a menu and this is where our problems started. There was a lot of conch on the menu, for anyone who doesn't know what conch is, well it's basically the snail thingie that lives in the beautiful pink shells which you see on sale everywhere in Nassau. Fried, boiled, raw, chowders, fritters, gumbo and a lot of other variations of conch. I personally have a rule that I won't eat something that I wouldn't step in so conch in any way shape or form was definitely off my menu. We cautiously chose from the menu, but when the meal arrived, we found weren't as in touch with eating like the locals as we had previously thought. Gristle and fat were plentiful on our plates and as much as we tried, we couldn't get used to the style of cooking.

On one particularly hot day, and after we had been for a walk we stopped once back in town, to go for a wander around the local market. It was one which featured ladies selling their hand made goods. Clothing, scarves, basket ware and jewellery. I started talking to a lady who was selling baskets that she had made herself. I was looking at the baskets and eventually chose a lovely one to use as a fruit basket when we got home. David had wandered off somewhere and I found him sitting having a cigar on a wall nearby.

Later that evening, we were back in the hotel, we dropped our shopping in the room and headed outside for a drink. We took off our shoes and wandered into the Caribbean Sea to cool off. Beautiful, crystal clean, bright blue water. As we were splashing and wandering about, David took my hand, reached for something out of his pocket and as he pushed a ring with a small scallop shell on my finger, he asked me to marry him!

What an amazing life this fat bird is living.

We flew home, fortunately not with any of the cabin crew we recognised from our hotel, but with me proudly wearing my scallop shell engagement ring. I have to add that, a few weeks later we did fly to Turkey for a long weekend to buy my real engagement ring which is truly magnificent. Following my amazing life in Turkey, my amazing life still continues. I am one of the luckiest women alive!

It Wasn't a Viennese Whirl, That's for Sure!

We love Christmas markets, and we have, in the years we have been together, been to quite a few. Each year when we return from our long weekend we are almost instantly planning where we will go the following year. We always plan our holidays like that if we can as I need to book holidays at work. We need to make sure David's schedule is blocked off, and we all need something to look forward to.

Vienna was on the radar this particular year, I had a friend from Austria when I lived in Turkey and she was always telling everyone how nice the country was, how nice the markets were. So, Vienna was the choice. We had chosen a lovely hotel, situated, according to the site we booked it through, very close to the biggest and most visited Christmas Market. This, the most popular market, is in front of the City Hall.

We flew into Vienna airport and took a taxi into the city and the hotel itself. It truly was in a great place, the centre of town, in a fine old building surrounded by lots of other equally fabulous buildings. Baroque, Gothic and every single one was so highly decorated and ornamental. We were only staying a couple of nights so we unpacked our clothing, put on an extra layer because it was absolutely freezing outside, and we headed outside as fast as we could.

It was early evening, and as I said, it was absolutely freezing already. As the sun started to settle, it became even colder. I have, over the years, collected several types of headgear bought from the cities we visit for their Christmas Markets. They are invariably the coldest places ever. I left the hotel in a very becoming knitted pink hat I had bought in Munich during another Christmas Market visit. It had ear flaps and a huge swathe of white 'fur' around my head. But, when spending several days outside, I had decided that having a warm head was more important than not looking stupid!

Our first port of call was to be the most advertised market in front of the City Hall. As we approached it, we could see the backdrop of the City Hall all lit up in its Christmas finery. That was wonderful, but the smells… ah the smells, candles, all manner of sweets, doughnuts, sausage, mulled wines. It was lovely, even from a distance, and as we got closer, we could see the little wooden huts all decorated with fairy lights selling all manner of food and drinks and handmade crafts. We wandered for a while, taking in all the smells and sights, and generally enjoying it all. We had a drink of mulled wine and checked out the City Hall. We didn't go in, but the ground floor was dedicated to children and they could make crafts such as Christmas Candles and cookies. Some days there were planned choirs there, singing Christmas carols. The whole thing was great and well worth the visit. Over the next couple of days, we checked this market out more than a few times. We bought drinks, food and Christmas items to hang on our tree at home.

As we left the market, we were hungry and as we wandered down one of the small streets radiating away from the market we stumbled onto an Irish Bar. We decided we were both happy to go 'Irish'. It was warm inside, and a friendly place with a good choice of pub foods which is what we particularly like, so it proved to be a good choice. In fact, we used the Irish Bar a couple of times during our stay in Vienna. After eating and thawing out we started back towards the hotel, but discovered that around every corner on the narrow streets there were tiny little markets, some just five or six little huts, but all worth having a look around. It took us ages to get back to the hotel, but I would recommend taking the time to check out all these little markets. Stand and have a mulled wine and doughnuts or a Bratwurst sausage.

The following day, we had booked a two-day ticket on the open top bus tours. The commentaries are always interesting and informative, so its well worth giving them a try for getting your bearings in any city.

We visited a couple of the markets, none of which should be missed if you ever get the chance to visit Vienna at this time of year. We visited the Belvedere Palace, taking in the baroque backdrop of this world-famous palace. Most of the markets sold similar wares, crafts, candles, Christmas baubles and the great little gnomes, who I'm sure will have special names, but you know the ones, long pointy hats and even longer beards. The food, with all its smells, and mulled wines, and wonderful hot chocolates. We visited Maria Thereisen Square and in the evening the Christmas Market at Spittleberg which is located on some of the narrow streets here, to find ceramics, jumpers, rugs, silver and enamel jewellery. On our visit I bought an apron! I know, not exactly cool, but I do use one for certain meals and this one was hand printed and extremely nice. We spoke to the lady selling them and she was part of a sect which sounded a little like the Amish, but whatever it was, they had a stall full of beautiful printed items. I still use the apron to this day.

We ended up as the day was winding down, back at the first market we visited at the City Hall. As we left the lights, the festive noise and the wonderful sites, we were once again drawn to the warm welcome in the Irish Bar. Trust me, we don't normally pick 'English' type bars and restaurants to eat in, it was purely serendipity. We tried Austrian bars during the day for a beer and hot chocolate, but eating is done while you are wandering around the markets. There's so much choice. And it would be rude not too.

On our second full day, we once again headed out from the hotel for much of the same, this time jumping on and off the tour bus and using it as a taxi. It was easy to find the bigger more popular markets, but in some places, it was just a case of walking around the corner and there would be another small market to browse. Everywhere we go I try to find something nice for the Christmas Tree and something small for the house. I found several little ornaments for the tree and couldn't resist a gnome to sit on the windowsill at Christmas.

But this day I was in a little pain. Thinking back I do think it was due to the extreme cold, as I really don't 'do' cold very well, even though I love the Christmas markets, but this year it was, and I mean it was, absolutely freezing. We didn't stay outside for too long without finding a nice bar to head into to warm up, me grabbing hot chocolates of many descriptions, many with alcohol or fruit flavours and for David to sample some of the fine craft beers.

My shins were, however, killing me. Occasional cramps, but just an unbearable pain which I was handling with painkillers. As we were heading back towards the hotel that evening David suggested we buy some form of oil or heat gel and he would rub my legs for me before we went to bed. I did think it might be a good idea, so we headed into a store which seemed to have items ranging from hair and body products to fragrances and aftershaves. We were clearly in the right sort of place, but we were also a little off the beaten track, and not very much of the signage was in English. No clues, so we wandered around, laughing, we were both reasonably intelligent people, how hard could it be to find a 'hot' rub?

Well very hard, it seemed, but after wandering for a while, and just as we started to get worried that we would have the store detective chasing us as shop lifters, we picked up a promising-looking tube of stuff and walked to the checkouts. The tube had pictures of leaves on it, but also something that looked like a suggestion for heat. It was a guess, but once we got outside, we opened the tube and it smelt minty, and most definitely hot.

Back at the hotel I had a hot shower and sat on the edge of the bed, David was really very happy to try and stop my legs hurting as we were travelling home the next day and he was a little worried about how I might react on the plane with the pressure. He put some of the cream on his hands, it was white and thick, a lot like the cream you would put on your baby if you had any issues at changing time. He rubbed both hands together and I asked him how it felt, was it hot? He did say it was warmish! He then started rubbing the cream onto the calf and shin on one of my legs. As he rubbed, it seemed to become more and more difficult to massage my leg. David rubbed until he kind of came to a halt, almost as if he had glued himself to my leg. We both started laughing but had no idea why he was sticking and slowing down! He pulled his hand away and stuck it under my nose and I instantly realised what the problem was. David was attempting to give me a leg massage using toothpaste! Another shower followed and boy did it take some doing to get all the toothpaste off my leg, and indeed off David's hands. We laughed, we laughed, and we laughed some more, that was certainly a first and I'm happy to say, a last! Irony is, my legs never hurt after that!

Now whenever I think of Vienna, of course I remember the wonderful city, we would like to visit in the summer to have another look around, as it is so spectacular. But I remember the toothpaste incident!

The Pissing Boy Who Couldn't

Every time David and I decide on a trip, I like to get onto the internet ahead of time and plan how many things we can squeeze in. Some people might argue with this way of travelling and I admit that if David and I were younger then we might do things differently, but as we grow older, we are unlikely to visit anywhere more than once as there are so many places we would like to see together so we really 'go for it'!

Our first Christmas market trip was to Brussels in Belgium. Until I met David, I really hadn't travelled to many European countries, I had been to Belgium for a five day trip when I was at school, but due to living in Turkey for such a long time and being married to Turks who couldn't easily travel, my travelling had been limited. To add to the fun, David and I decided to travel on the Eurostar which was another first for me, and I was truly excited.

I looked up the city, the history, saw the amazing buildings, the previously held Christmas markets. From the hotel's location it was easy to get to the bigger markets, but far enough away not to be in the middle of all the noise and people wandering around. I was so happy. I made a list of things I'd love for us to visit if we got the chance. I still do this with every trip, we don't always see them all, but we do pretty well, and David is such a great husband. Even though a lot of the places we visit he has already been to over the years he's been working around the world, he is still happy to take me, accompany me, and sometimes just enjoy watching me when I am amazed at something, and smile with joy.

The list I had for Brussels was to see the Grand Place, which is a big marketplace surrounded by amazing buildings which were the Guild Halls. The Atomium, which is like something from Men in Black, but is in fact a Steel sculpture of an Atom (a very, very, large Atom). But THE thing I wanted to see, apart from the Christmas Markets, was the Mannikin Pis. This, quite literally translated, is 'The Peeing Boy' but he is also fondly known as The Pissing Boy and as I'm not always Politically Correct, then that's what he was to me!

I liked this little statue. Like most people, I'd seen pictures of him, but I was interested in why he was in Brussels pissing into a fountain at all, it's not your normal sort of statue, is it? There are a few accounts which I will share with you as to why he is there. One is that a little boy was caught peeing on a witch's doorstep, and she turned him into a statue, vowing that he would have a full bladder and need to pee forever. Another is that a little boy peed on a burning fuse which led to a stash of hidden gunpowder from enemies of Brussels who had pretended to retreat but had hidden the explosives. The city made the statue out of gratitude.

The last, which is my favourite, is that the statue was in gratitude to the tanning industry in Belgium, which had a huge tanning industry. It was not unusual to have children peeing on the leather as the ammonia in pee helps to make the leather more supple. I smile when I imagine hundreds of kids peeing on leather! There are others, but you'll have to take to the internet and have a read for yourself if you're really interested.

There have been several statues as well. Apparently, he's been stolen and replaced several times, and at one such theft, he was snapped off at the ankles!

I also learned that the Pissing Boy has a lot of little outfits that he is sometimes dressed up in for special occasions, which I found odd, but hey ho, Belgians put mayonnaise on chips, so they probably have lots of little odd habits. His modern outfits include Santa Claus and Mickey Mouse. I find it a little insulting that such an iconic thing would be dressed up, but hey, that's just my opinion.

Anyhow, back to the trip. As the day approached, I started packing the overnight bags, and I'm dreadful when it comes to holiday or trip packing. I always start too early, change my mind a lot, then I panic in case I haven't packed the right things, so I sometimes unpack and repack! But we get there in the end and I'm always OK with the weight of the cases if we are flying. David was used to travelling very light before he met me, so I think he is often traumatised when I start! When he's travelling alone for work, he literally starts to pack fifteen minutes before he has to leave the house!

We headed out from our local train station, and even travelling on a train is exciting for me as I just never did it in the past. For me the fun started when we were on the platform. The train was coming in on a different platform, so there is a bridge to cross to get to it. Bear in mind I'm a big bird, but I can still move, I can walk very well, I can even trot for a short distance, but that can't be combined with steep stairs, dashing and carrying a professionally packed overnight case AND a handbag. Pfff men have no idea sometimes!

David, once he knew where we needed to be, was off like a bloody rocket. He has far too much energy for a man of his age and was used to doing this as he's been travelling somewhere over half of his life. But he also has longer legs than me, a smaller lighter bottom and belly and no handbag, so of course he was already a hundred metres in front of me. As I was halfway up the steps, he's up, over the bridge and heading down to the platform where the train was. I'm trying my best to keep up but when he shouts at me with a very strange Yorkshire accent, 'Come on, Love!!' I crack up and get him slightly cross as I am, in his words buggering about! To explain this, David, doesn't have a Yorkshire Accent, he has no accent, he speaks very nicely with no hint of anything. So the Yorkshire accent just sent me into fits of laughter, I didn't know where it came from and then to be told when we got settled on the train, the train that we didn't miss by the way, that I was buggering about that much that we might have missed the train! The cheek! I laughed a lot on that train journey! We had only known each other for about nine months, and living together for a few short weeks, so I knew my life was changing for the better, with lots of love and laughter. Lots.

We arrived at Kings Cross Station in London and from there it's just a quick walk across the road and into St Pancras. Through the shopping mall and the random man playing the piano which is there for random people to use. Then to the Eurostar terminal, a quick check in, and then grab a seat for a coffee and beer. Up to the platform when the time is right and onto the train. It's easy, comfortable, less stressful and I love it. We speed along, chatting, eating, drinking, laughing, under the tunnel which I thought might freak me out but it never, then watching the changed scenery emerge. Before we knew it, we are arriving in Brussels, off the train, through the station and out into the city.

We use David's sat nav qualifications to walk to the hotel! I think due to the earlier buggering about that he took us on the long route, but we arrived at a lovely hotel frontage. However, due to an horrific terrorist attack in Paris earlier that year, there were armed soldiers guarding the door. The Warwick, highly recommended to anyone visiting Brussels.

The hotel was in a great place. The following day, after breakfast, we set off on our Brussels adventure. We walked a fair way, but all easy walking, mainly along cobbled streets. On both sides of the roads were great looking shops with chocolate, waffles and many various food items. The smells were wonderful. After a couple of hours of exploring we found a nice little café and sat outside. I experienced my first fruit beer! I rarely drink nowadays, but if I lived in Belgium, I would undoubtedly be an alcoholic. Fruit beer is phenomenal! They taste great, almost like drinking a glass of pop. We looked for this when we were back in the UK. It was available, but because it's not local it was very expensive. That's one reason why I'm not alcoholic.

Afterwards we headed off and found the first of the many Christmas markets scattered throughout the city. I love Christmas markets, the smells, the sounds, the lights and the wonderful rows of little cabins, full of everything from gnomes with long beards to jewellery, candles and sweets. There's chocolate, and oh, everything else you can imagine there should be, such as stalls selling bratwurst sausage, selling local delicacies, mulled wine, hot chocolate with whipped cream on the top. On this market David found something he loved, which was warm Amaretto. When we are at these Christmas markets, I never really know how David can walk for the whole day without falling over blind drunk! But it seems that the alcohol hardly touches him, maybe it is being outside in the cold? Maybe he just has the constitution of a large horse, he never gets hangovers either!

At the back of the Market there was a Ferris Wheel, a humongous, big bastard of a Ferris wheel. Bear in mind that David and I were still learning about each other. We approached it and David was all for having a ride, I smiled and said, 'yes of course, it will be fun'. Ha! I'm actually very scared of heights, but there was no way I was prepared at this stage of our relationship to admit it. So…. we stepped up to the ticket booth and David bought two tickets, we then walked along a platform waiting for the next cage to stop and empty out before we stepped in. They were literally like cages, and once you were in there was no seat harness or safety anything, no parachute, nothing! Just wooden seats on both side and two tiny doors, one on each end of the cage. I would have pointed out there and then that I didn't think the Health and Safety man looking after the ride had looked at it for years, but I decided to be brave! I actually did very well and managed to smile and look as if I was having a great time.

However, once we left the ground my façade crumbled, and I grabbed the side of the cage quite firmly. My knuckles were hurting as I was holding on so tight. David was having a great time, pointing out things on the ground and in the market, things we hadn't seen yet. I had a peep but was more interested in the approaching roof of a building. I was terrified, but still really trying to be cool about being what felt like thousands of feet above the ground, in a cage with no safety harness or parachute. It was at this point that David realised I was having difficulties. Being the nice guy he is, he didn't try to console me or make me feel better in a way that might have actually made me feel better. Instead, he stood up and started jumping up and down and then he actually danced! His way of making me feel better about being thousands of feet in the air was to Dad-dance, in an attempt to prove that the cage was structurally very safe. As an engineer, I'm sure he thought that was a good visual, I'm sure he thought he was helping but I'm not an engineer, and it didn't.

Needless to say, by the time the bloody wheel of death had gone around and around and around at least three hundred and twelve times and was finally stopping to let us out I was a bag of jelly! We left the wheel and headed directly for something alcoholic and this time I didn't refuse and go for the hot chocolate option! Strangely enough, in the years we have been together, there is always something, almost everywhere we go, that means I have to try and put my fear of heights in my pocket. Cable cars by the dozen, all over the world, a helicopter ride, and a hot air balloon ride. But so far, I have made it back to earth and I haven't embarrassed myself by peeing out of fear or vomiting when watching the earth get further and further away. I think heights might be one of the few things I'm scared of. Just saying, David!

We had great fun, in and around the markets in Brussels. As seems to be the way with these markets, they appear around corners, everyone is so friendly, and they are just a happy joyous thing to be part of. That evening, once it was dark, we were wandering around the markets and lovely cobble streets and saw people making their way down a small alley between the buildings. So, we followed, of course. When we got to the other end of the alley it opened up into a lovely big square with cafes and restaurants and shops most of the way round, and a huge Christmas Tree lit up in the centre. As we checked out the shops and cafes a fabulous light show started. It was lighting up the side of one of the biggest buildings on the square and was like nothing I've seen before. We stood and watched the show, marvelling at the sight before heading back to the hotel.

Once back at the hotel, we decided on a night cap in the inviting bar next to the reception area. It was dark and moody and once inside we saw a grand piano being played. We grabbed a drink and found comfy seats at the back of the bar where we were out of anyone's way and sat to thaw out and enjoy our drinks and each other. Shoes off, feet up and drinks in hand. Then we heard a noise, a noise that didn't sound real, something from the radio or a TV? But no, it was emanating from a girl, maybe in her mid-twenties. The odd sound was her laughter, it was a mix of a machine gun, someone trying really hard to imitate a horse and definitely someone out of control! It was the funniest laugh ever. David and I spent the next hour sipping our drinks and laughing at the horse girl. She was truly formidable.

Now to finish off this little Brussels adventure. Remember my to-see list at the beginning of the story? Well we had seen the Market Place and all the magnificent buildings located on or around it. We never got to see the Atom statue, but on our last day I asked David if we could go and find the Pissing Boy. It wasn't far from the hotel, and it didn't take us a long time to find him. But oh, what a disappointment. There he was, snuggled onto a corner, surrounded by waffles and chocolate shops, all with copies of him in their window displays, just as we had been seeing all over Brussels. There were thousands of copies of him, big and small, everywhere. But to find him squished between the waffle shop and souvenir shops was disappointing. It would have been easy to walk pass and miss him! However, we had found him, the Pissing Boy of Brussels, the little iconic statue known around the world by millions of people. But he wasn't pissing. In fact, it was impossible to see him. From head to toe there was some very strange beige crocheted/knitted wool 'thing' covering him. No signs anywhere explaining anything, no crowds of people taking pictures, for obvious reasons and the biggest let down ever. We found out when we arrived home and had the time to get onto the internet, but this monstrosity of a knitted 'thing' was supposed to represent a condom and the poor little bugger was dressed in it for World Aid's Day. I look back now and I've just checked him out on the net and I can laugh now, I can laugh a lot, but the poor pissing boy couldn't, and he wasn't even pissing during our visit!

To Russia With a Lover

Amongst our adventures, I'm very pleased to say David and I were lucky enough to visit Russia. Our plan was St Petersburg, in the past known at Petrograd or Leningrad. Never in my life would I have ever considered visiting Russia, but David convinced me that it was easily doable! Ok then, I'm up for it.

Now it didn't turn out to be quite as easy as we thought. The first obstacle thrown at us was obtaining a visa to enable us to enter Russia. This involved a trip to London to the visa office, not a consulate, just the office of a company that had been established to issue visas.

We decided to combine two things to save money and David's precious time. During that time David was incredibly busy at work and was travelling all over the world, getting home just for weekends if we were lucky. So, we combined this trip to the visa office with a trip to Paris on the Eurostar, the plan was to get off the Eurostar on the way home, stay overnight in London and then visit the Russian Visa office the following day before catching the train home. Sounded like a plan.

On the day we travelled back to London from Paris we clambered from the train and dashed through the station. I'm never quite sure why David expects me to dash every time we are in some form of a station, be it a train station or an airport. I get the point if we are running late, but we are rarely late as my husband is THE best travel planner ever. I'm not really built for dashing, but I try my best, sometimes however I just give up and stop, then I wait until David realises that I'm not actually puffing and panting next to him. It can take a while sometimes, as he is clearly on a mission, but when he realises and turns to look for me, he never says anything, but smiles and then slows down.

So, we are out of St Pancras, or St Pancreas as I always seem to call it, and heading across the road, looking for the hotel we are staying the night in. Bear in mind, we were living the life at that period in time, David was travelling lots and collecting vast quantities of points from various places and airlines. We were able to turn these points into hotel stays, he also stayed in a chain of hotels in the US which was a distant relation of the Hilton Group, and he collected Hilton-Honours points, which meant we could stay in Hiltons using the points instead of cash. We were spoiled in regard to the hotels we stayed in on our travels, for sure. However, this night was to put us to the test of roughing it! We found the hotel, just a ten-minute walk from the train station and we hoped, if David's calculations were correct, that it would only be forty-minute walk from the Visa office. We entered the tiny reception area, and I mean tiny, it was very similar to the room Harry Potter had under the stairs at Privet Close, but the guy was welcoming, and it was very clean. We were told where our room was, and we travelled up in a tiny lift to the correct floor. It did seem that the building had possibly fifteen thousand rooms, because the landing we got off at was just doors. No walls, just doors. Could it be that the rooms were just the width of the doors?

We found our room and I do believe we were lucky, since it was a corner room. That meant we were able to turn around in the room, but only just, only in one direction and only one at a time! The room was clean and tidy but so, so, tiny. The word 'bijou' doesn't even come close. The bed was pushed against a wall that had a window. Across from the bed was a wardrobe designed for barbie, and the bathroom was from the same range of small designers. We laughed and commented about the fall of the mighty! But we were so tired. David took a picture from the window or the wonderful buildings across the road from the hotel. It was dark outside and had been snowing. It was a wonderful sight.

We had set an alarm for the morning as we had a strict appointment at the visa office, and we wanted to leave our weekend luggage at the left-luggage office in King Cross so we didn't have to carry it about for the morning.

We woke and made ourselves ready for the day to come. We went downstairs for breakfast, not quite sure what to expect and were directed into the basement, surprised to find a nice little seating area. We were serviced with a basic but nice breakfast. Several coffees later we left the hotel and as we opened the door to step out onto the pavement, we were stunned to see that everything was covered with a, now heavy, coat of snow!

Nevertheless, we walked as swiftly as we were able to King's Cross and to the luggage office to store our bags. Once they were safely stored we set off to the visa office. This was made harder by the fact that not only were we heading up a hill, but it was slippery due to the snow and hidden ice. It took us longer than we had expected, but an hour later we were standing outside the daunting looking visa office. We went through security and a huge door which was opened once we explained we had an appointment. Once inside, there was more security and a bag check, then we were asked to take a seat. Bang on time our name was called, and we approached the counter to be faced with a stern looking middle-aged lady. She checked our names, took our passports off us and instructed me to 'sit', which I did! She spoke with David for a few minutes and then he returned to sit next to me. She waved me back to the counter, asked me a few questions and then gave me the 'sit' instruction again. In most places I would have made David laugh with a few comments and observations, but this was definitely not the place to do that, so we both sat, like we were naughty kids outside the headmaster's office. Another few minutes passed, then we were both called to the counter and handed our passports back, happily with visa's stuck inside!

OK, stage one of our Russian Adventure was in the bag! Would everyone in Russia be like that lady? We headed home pleased with the visa's we had tucked in our passports, and excited at the thought of the long weekend in St Petersburg to come.

The long weekend arrived. We were visiting Russia a couple of months prior to the World Cup and we weren't sure if this was a good thing or not. We were soon to find out. We had a good flight, it lasted about three and a half hours from Heathrow direct into St Petersburg. St Petersburg was a busy airport, and we had a queue to reach the passport control area, but once there, it went fairly quickly, and before we knew it, we were standing outside the terminal building. We'd already ascertained that it was about a thirty-minute car ride into St Petersburg and to the hotel, so we grabbed a taxi, threw our bags in the boot and were on our way.

We were surprised. Russia wasn't quite what we expected. The streets seemed to be incredibly clean, in my mind I'd expected copious amounts of graffiti, so it shows how wrong I was. We arrived at the hotel, which was charming, a great reception area with nice friendly staff. The hotel turned out to be very quirky which we loved. No lifts, but several floors all with unusual decoration, quirky looking doorways and a variety of furniture on the landings and areas between rooms where there was floor space. We loved it. The room was large and comfortable and although we hadn't realised or booked that weekend on purpose, we had arrived on a weekend when there were celebrations for Peter the Great. We had also learned, before we arrived, that the time of year we going to be there was known as 'white nights' and the sun seems to never fully set over St Petersburg.

Breakfast was served in a restaurant belonging to and attached to the hotel. It was a very pleasant meal, eaten in an old fashioned but truly quirky restaurant.

For two days, David and I walked miles through St Petersburg. A truly wonderful, clean, friendly place. There were beautiful hanging baskets and floral decorations everywhere. There were enormous queues for the iconic places, and we rarely queue as there is far too much to visit and see on long weekends. But we arrived at The Church of the Saviour on the Spilled Blood. This is an absolutely amazing, mind blowing structure, situated on the side of Griboyedov canal, with globes and towers of bright colours and gold. We joined the queue and entered. Seven thousand five hundred square meters of mosaics greeted us, and we both wandered around taking photos and remaining in awe of such a spectacular site.

We wandered by the State Hermitage Museum, but unfortunately the queue was probably close to twelve miles long. We walked several times by the amazing Winter Palace and all its glory. Since it was a celebration of Peter the Great the weekend we visited, stages and screens were being erected and the place was buzzing with activity and excitement. We walked along the Palace embankment, we roamed the Botanical Gardens. We walked over the Palace Bridge over the River Neva onto Hare island to the Peter and Paul Cathedral and were surprised to see a beach area, which was full of sun bathers and people swimming. This bridge is left open to allow shipping to pass during the night, making moving about St Petersburg difficult if not impossible.

This city was so extraordinary, palaces, museums, huge formal squares, churches and then we found Nevsky Avenue, the main road running through the city. Here we found shop after shop, full of Russian nested dolls, the brightly painted wooden dolls that tuck away inside themselves, and of course we bought several sets, both as presents and for ourselves. The colour, choice and workmanship were breath taking when they were all in one place.

This was certainly a place that couldn't, even with the best planning, be seen in just a few days. There is a staggering amount of history, but we were really so pleased we made the trip.

We found a great pub which served great meals and it was just off Nevsky Avenue. So, from our table outside we could see the street entertainers and the hustle and bustle of people. But the odd thing we encountered? There always has to be at least one every time we have an adventure.

This one occurred following our visit to St Isaacs Cathedral. St Isaacs has a huge golden dome and was very impressive, set next to a beautifully laid out and presented garden. Across the road we spotted a Pizza restaurant. Now, I'm not a big pizza lover but David is, and I can always find something I like so we headed in. Pizza is surely Pizza in any country or any language, isn't it? Anyway, I ordered cannelloni and David chose a simple Margarita Pizza. The meal arrived, nice polite helpful waiter, busy place, but our meal came out quite quickly and was placed on nice spotlessly clean white tablecloths. We both tucked in but after a couple of minutes David asked me to check his Pizza out! Eh? But he pointed something out and when I checked he was right, there was a pizza base, there was melted cheese and slices of tomato. But it looked a little dry and the reason? No tomato paste on the base! To this day, we don't know if that was a speciality of the restaurant, a mistake, or the way Russians like Pizza. We will never know, as we didn't say anything. I laughed my way through the rest of our meal and David muttered and picked his way through his Pizza.

Apart from strange Pizzas, we would both recommend a visit to St Petersburg. The history, bedecked in flowers at every turn, the beautifully clean pavements and squares. And if you visit at the right time of year, it doesn't get dark so you can stay out sightseeing as long as your legs will hold you up! We are truly lucky people to have visited such an astonishing place, well worth the painful trip to the Visa Office, especially if that lady is still behind the desk there!

A Toboggan Ride

Oh yes, I've done that as well! Hard to believe that fat birds toboggan, but this isn't a story of me running behind a toboggan, dressed in tight fitting leggings and a crash helmet and then finally jumping in the thing as it speeds down through the snow! This is a story of me climbing into a toboggan that basically consisted of a wicker basket, with my husband seated next to me. Two wooden slats were strapped underneath the basket, for sliding on, and two brave men standing behind us. How did we get there, I hear you asking, so OK I'll explain.

We were on a plane travelling back from a weekend break visiting a Christmas market somewhere cold, I think it was Vienna. I just happened to mention that it was a shame that all the Christmas markets were held where it was freezing cold. A year later we were on another plane heading towards Madeira, why? Well David had investigated and had found that in Funchal, the biggest city on Madeira, they also held Christmas Fayres, and trimmed up the city with lights. And it would be warm in December. We were on our way!

Funchal was a wonderful place. It seemed like every building and tree in the centre had lights strung on it. They were some of the best lights we have seen during our travels to Christmas Fayres. There was a park that had little cabins, and a small train running through a Christmas village. Around most corners there were choirs and sculptures. In one special part of the town centre there was an outdoor stage where different school choirs performed during each day. All the little ones dressed in their uniforms, so smart, and so proud. We stopped each evening to watch whichever school were performing.

The people were very welcoming, the food was great. The Christmas market itself was small but really good. The lights were fantastic, but that wasn't the end of it. When I was doing my normal investigations, I found a few unusual things to see and do. One particular day we went off to explore. We walked along the harbour front until we came to a cable car station. Yep you heard me correctly, once again I was risking life and limb hanging from a thread to visit the top of a mountain, which in this case backs onto Funchal.

But, very fortunately as it turned out, before we reached the station a young man approached us. He was a taxi driver, and he explained how he could save us money and that, by using his services we could see a lot more of Madeira to boot. It really did work out like that. His plan worked liked this. He would take us up to the Botanical gardens, come back two hours later and collect us at the gate. He would then transfer us over to the start of the toboggan ride. After that, he would collect us from the end of the ride and then take us to the top station of the cable car, which we would take to come back down! This all sounds a bit barmy, but these places were high up and the mountains have a ravine between the botanical gardens and the toboggan ride. One way to cross it is using another cable car but doing it that way by ourselves would have costs us a lot more in time and money.

Plus, it saved me doing a ride up in the cable car! Winner, winner here! We climbed into the taxi; the driver pointed out the number on the side to make sure we didn't climb into anyone else's Taxi during the rest of this day, I guess. And we were off. The scenery travelling up to the Botanical garden's wasn't spectacular, it was mainly housing and businesses, but we could see a couple of cable cars trundling up and down and we did see the ravine as we went over it in the taxi.

We were dropped off outside the botanical gardens and given instructions as to where we would exit and where the taxi would be waiting. We paid to get in, and once in the gardens, it was an absolute riot of colour and unusual plants. Cacti bigger than I'd ever seen, and for me the best thing was the Birds of Paradise flowers. I'd once been given one by an admirer. That was the first time I had seen ever seen them in reality, so seeing them here growing everywhere was fantastic. We wandered the gardens, found a little café and sat and had a drink, enjoying the winter sunshine. This place was a great for spending a few days getting away from the cold and rain of the UK.

We roamed back through the gardens until we found the Exit gates. We went through the turnstiles and were out onto the road. We quickly found our taxi and driver and were now being whisked off to toboggan. We now understood why this taxi had saved us money, it saved us another Cable Car ride across to the toboggan. We were up and down the hills; we drove past the cable car station and another mile around the bendy roads until we stopped. We stopped seemingly in the middle of nowhere. The driver pointed towards a small alley and we set off, really, REALLY unsure of what was waiting for us.

We walked around the corner and were faced with lots of men, all dressed in white trousers and tops, all wearing boater style hats and coloured sashes around their waists. Behind them, we were just in time to see a wicker basket, with a couple sitting in it, set off down the hill in front of them. Two guys dressed in white were running down the road behind the toboggan, each holding onto a rope fastened to it! They ran at first to get the toboggan going, then when it was going fast enough, they jumped onto the back of it! When it was going what seemed extremely fast, they jumped off. At this point they used their bodies to slow and steer it. Their shoes had been soled with old tyre rubber to provide the grip needed.

Now, I had seen a picture of this toboggan on Facebook. It was of a friend I went to school with, Jo, and her husband Clive. Hi Jo if you're reading. But the picture of them seated in the basket gave no indication of the horrors involved. They looked so calm! David bought the ticket, and whilst he was doing that I was helped into the next toboggan at the top of the hill. I asked one of the guys where the brake was, and he showed me the sole of his shoes and laughed. Mmmm, OK!

David climbed in. Our guys rocked the toboggan and then pushed it forward. Before very long we were travelling terrifyingly quickly, and our guys were pulling and steering with the ropes and jumping on and off to speed us up and slow us down. The tarmac in front of us was very shiny and it was easy to see that so many toboggans had clearly whizzed down this road before us. I looked it up when we got home, and people have been doing this for over a hundred years!

At certain places the guys jumped on the back and a photographer would pop up from a garden or behind a wall and take a photo of us whizzing past. There were two really scary parts of this dash. The first was when we came to a part of the road that had brick walls on both sides. We went particularly fast there, and at the same time the basket turned through ninety degrees and we seemed to be going sideways! As we straightened up, there, right in front of us, was a crossroads. There was a man standing in the middle with a paddle thing in his hands. He had no chance of stopping us, but hopefully the people driving round these roads were all used to these odd people zipping past!

It was a fabulous ride though. The guys were super cool, and we arrived at the bottom of the road safe, sound and exhilarated. A man appeared offering to sell us one of the photos that had been taken as we sped past, it had been put inside a folder showing photos of people from many years ago doing the same thing. As we walked down a flight of steps to where the taxis were parked up, we saw the baskets being lifted onto trucks and the, what shall we call them? The gondoliers, climbing aboard a bus to take them all back to the top. What a way to earn a living! And how many times did they need their shoes re-soling?

We jumped back into our waiting taxi once more, and within a few minutes we were standing outside the cable car station. Phew it was all go that day, and we were still alive! But we still had the cable car to go. Once again, we were paying to sit in a goldfish bowl and be dangled from a thread whilst we travelled over ravines!

Before we set off down the cable car, we had seen a shop. I just can't walk past souvenir shops without breaking into hives, so we nipped in for a look. We ended up buying a bottle of Madeira wine, which seemed suitable bearing in mind where we were. And of course, a Wicker Toboggan fridge magnet. We stepped into the moving cable car. I was very adept at this now. Another couple climbed in behind us, and they helped fill the journey. They seemed to have done everything, travelled everywhere and seen everything. We couldn't understand why they were even there! But we reached the bottom, still alive once again. What a day that had been!

We walked back towards the city centre. Now, this bit is odd, but I need to share it as I always do Neither David nor I particularly like pigeons. I wouldn't hurt them if I can help it, but they make such a mess and we happened to have been fighting a losing battle with pigeons in a tree in our garden.

We were walking along a wide pavement. In front of us there were dozens of pigeons, sitting right in the way and clearly not in any mood to move. David had the Madeira wine in a carrier bag in his hand. He swung his arm and made a noise designed to shoo the pigeons away. It was something like a Yorkshire farmer would say, so I had rubbed off on his vocabulary. His noise was like Geeeeeeeee-onnnnnnn! The moment he swung his arm up, the carrier bag came apart and the wine flew higher than the pigeons. It came back down and hit the floor with a strange noise. It splashed upwards and we were both covered in sticky Madeira wine. We looked at the carrier bag remains in his hand. The handle was like a D shape, still over his knuckles and in his hand, but nothing else. The rest of the bag was gone!

We cleaned up the glass from the bottle, most of which had stayed in the bulk of the bag. We went off for a drink, not Madeira wine I hasten to add.

We had gotten through a dangerous day and were still laughing!

Up, Up and away…

I lived in Turkey for many years, ten to be precise, and I was lucky enough to travel a lot of Turkey. I travelled to the Syrian border, even sneaked across into Aleppo. I travelled almost as far north as the Black Sea, but never quite managed to reach the coast. I've spent time in Istanbul, an amazing place, and one which I'm guessing, you could visit dozens of times and still never see all of its wonders. I've seen the sunflower fields near Afyon which seemingly go on forever. I've seen the fields of Crocus heading up towards the Black Sea. I've seen the Whirling Dervishes, I've even seen the oiled up Turkish wrestlers. But I was only able to visit Cappadocia en-route to somewhere else, and never got to see as much of it as I'd wanted.

Last year David and I decided to put that right. We flew to Istanbul and had a wonderful few days roaming around. W stayed in a lovely little hotel literally round the corner from The Blue Mosque and the Byzantine Hagia Sophia Mosque. We were able to walk to the Topkapi Palace and The Grand Bazaar, which can keep you interested and entranced for hours. We ate some of the amazing food Turkey has to offer, we sat in cafes watching the very busy world of Istanbul go past. We took the open top bus tour and travelled through the city and over the Bosporus on a bridge that took us close by the Galata Tower and up to Taxim Square. We walked through the square and down Istiklal Caddesi, a long shopping street with nostalgic trams running along it.

All was going well on our long weekend until the rain came. It started when we were on Istiklal Caddesi, and it didn't know when to stop! We headed back up to jump on the next open bus tour double decker. There was one waiting and the staff had pulled down a plastic window/screen around the top deck, so we sat shivering amidst the absolute downpour that was taking place. This was August, and this was something we really hadn't expected, and certainly weren't dressed for!

The bus wasn't leaving anytime soon, as the tour personnel told us the rain was too bad to drive through. We sat about forty-five minutes shivering before the rain eased slightly, enough for the driver to feel confident to drive again. We headed off back towards the old part of Istanbul and our hotel. We passed flooded pavements and drove through flooded roads; it was chaos on the roads. The bus was moving very slowly and it had stopped raining now, so when David recognised where we were, we decided to jump off the bus and walk the rest of the way, as it would probably be quicker.

Now, I'd lived in Turkey for ten years, and I'd seen how heavy the rain can fall, but this was a surprise even to me. The bus driver had given us a plastic poncho with a hood, it was very attractive. But never was anything so useful. We set off walking, but the rain started again, not so heavy but it was constant and unforgiving. That morning, I'd gone out with sandals on, a comfortable unusual pair of sandals I'd bought on a previous trip to Alanya. They were made from rope, and as I was quite literally up to my ankles when we were crossing roads, my sandals were shrinking whilst on my feet! The water was flowing like a river down the hills and eventually we arrived back at our hotel, we looked like two drown rats, but once inside our room, we laughed at the situation we had been in. I was never able to wear my sandals again though.

We had a great little hotel in Istanbul, located in a great place. But we were leaving the next day, we would be heading to the airport and catching a flight to Kayseri Airport, which is one of the two airports that service the Cappadocia region. But first, we had organised an afternoon tour of the Basilica Cistern which was underground near the Blue Mosque. We loved the cistern; it was both amazing and interesting. It was lit well, giving it quite a spooky atmosphere. It features in the James Bond movie 'From Russia With Love' and the Dan Brown movie 'Inferno' amongst others. The cistern is one of hundreds which lie below Istanbul and it was built in the 6th century in the reign of Byzantine Emperor Justinian I. What was interesting was that the hundreds of columns in this underground world were mismatched, the entire place had been built with columns robbed and salvaged from other buildings. It was an amazing place and I'm really pleased we visited it. Well worth the visit if you get to Istanbul and have the time. The doorway is almost directly opposite the Hagia Sophia Mosque, easy to walk past if you're not looking for it.

We ate that evening in a restaurant just a few hundred metres from our hotel, a nice restaurant, but the star that evening was a little Jack Russel type dog. We were sitting opposite the doorway to a Turkish Baths, and a young guy came out with the biggest bundle of laundry in his arms, he balanced it on the moped parked at the kerbside and climbed on so that the laundry was between his legs and pushing up to the handle bars. That looked dangerous enough but then this funny little dog came running out of the Turkish Baths and jumped up onto the top of the laundry, he stood there as if he'd done it a million times before, and it was so funny. He looked like the boss! Everyone took his photo and he seemed to be posing. He then set off at quite a speed and vanished into the traffic, leaving everyone smiling at the little wonder dog!

Next morning, we were up early and away to the airport. We had booked with Pegasus, and I have to say, we would never fly with them again. It was chaos in the airport, even by Turkish standards. In both directions. Everyone travelling with Pegasus were at the same check in desks, there was the normal snaking queue, but so many people were pushing in and queue jumping, and there was bickering in the queue and out and out arguments with one particular member of staff who seemed to let large amounts of people queue jump if she liked the look of them! When we arrived a few days earlier into Istanbul, Pegasus had misplaced some of our luggage and were no help at all, and now we were queuing in the most chaotic muddle ever. Worst airline ever, after BA. David works with someone in Germany whose parents are Turkish, and when David told him before the trip that we were flying with Pegasus he smiled and said, 'you won't do it twice'.

After all this chaos we were eventually directed to the gate we were leaving from. Almost as much chaos there, as all the doors were locked and we couldn't get out of the tiny room we had been directed to. We were all let out in time to board the plane!

On arrival at Kayseri Airport, we left the plane and walked to the terminal. Now we were locked out of the terminal, on the runway! But they didn't lose any of our luggage this time, so that was a bonus, I guess. We had arranged for the hotel in Goreme we were staying at to take care of our transfer. Cappadocia has eight separate regions, and we chose Goreme because the hotel looked fabulous, and we had pre-booked a hot air balloon ride. The hotel was also very close to the Goreme open air museum which we wanted to see, and a short car ride from some of the underground cities that were scattered around Cappadocia.

We had a longer transfer than anticipated, but the weather was pleasant and the views good. We arrived at our hotel and had a wonderful surprise. We checked in and were shown to our room, which was massive. We were on the corner of the first floor, we had windows around most of the room and wonderful furniture. The bathroom was another surprise, the shower was big enough for a whole family to go in together! We had a walk around the hotel, and it was one pleasant surprise after another. We went to the roof, where the restaurant which would be serving breakfast was situated. It had an indoor section and an outside area with a canopy. Further along the roof were various seating areas with huge cushions. The view from the roof was breath taking, the scenery in Cappadocia is second to none.

If you have never heard of or seen pictures of this part of the world, have a look. Over the years, the soft volcanic rock has been moulded into pillars, cones and 'fairy chimneys'. There are caves throughout all of these, where people lived. There are churches and some of the underground cave systems form cities which can be visited and are now museums. It isn't easy to get to because it's inland, but if you are on holiday on the coast you can find two to three day tours that go there, or you can fly into Kayseri if you want to spend more time in Cappadocia, which I highly recommend.

We settled into our room, unpacked and then headed off for a walk to see what the town of Goreme had waiting. We walked the length of the main road. As expected, it is scattered with restaurants, shops, car hire places, and bars. We found a great little restaurant tucked away down a few stairs on the main road. The nice man who owned it served us a lovely meal, and David tried the local Cappadocia wine, which he was very happy with. This restaurant became our go-to restaurant for the few days we were there. We also found a little cocktail bar which was upstairs from a shop and was a great people watching base.

However, the first evening we were in Goreme, the bloody rain followed us. As we were strolling back to the hotel that first evening, the unrelenting heavy rain started, and once again we were rocking the 'drowned rat' look. But at least my sandals weren't in danger of needing to be cut off, these ones didn't shrink!

Now, when we plan holidays, David pays for a lot of it, but I give him cash before we leave towards the meals etc, and I always try to pre-book things that I can pay for. In Istanbul, I'd pre-booked the open top bus tour, and I bought a carpet to bring home. For this part of our holiday, I had booked us a Hot Air Balloon ride! When I read up about these flights, the biggest tip from reviews and sites was to book it for the first morning after you arrive in Cappadocia, as due to the weather they don't always fly. If you book it for your last morning, and that happens, then you're basically screwed. Following that advice, I had booked for the next morning. As we entered the reception, we asked the charming people on reception if they could contact the balloon company and ask what was happening now that the heavens had once again opened.

At that stage, I'm not 100% sure that I would have minded so much if it had been cancelled. After I'd booked the trip, I started watching videos on the internet about these flights. Bearing in mind I'm the fat bird on the cover, I had become a little paranoid, not about the balloon flight itself, although I really don't like heights, in fact hey frighten me to death. No, as a fat bird I was worried about climbing in, and then climbing out of the balloon basket! By the time we arrived in Turkey I had seen videos of many fat people being man-handled into baskets, I'd seen many cellulite loaded things trying desperate to straddle the top of the basket, many failing. I'd seen many fat bottoms of men and women all using different techniques to get in whilst remaining cool, whilst cracking some inappropriate joke and continuing to smile. Then no doubt worrying for the whole flight that they would have the same issue when it landed.

The receptionist kindly called the Balloon people who advised us to be outside the hotel at 4.30am as planned, they would collect us and take it from there depending on the weather. Bugger!

The next morning, David and I were up and ready and standing outside the hotel at 4.30 as planned. I've never seen so much activity at that time of a morning before. We were busy talking to the hotel dog, a huge monster of a dog. A Kangal, a particularly large dog which, in the centre of Turkey, is used as a guard dog/herder. This dog however wasn't expected to work, I think he'd retired as all he did was wander around during the day to keep out of the sun. Early mornings he would lounge about outside the hotel. His special thing, however, was to howl when the mosque call started. He howled along with the call to prayer until the call ended, at which point he would lay his head back down and go back to sleep. He was great, that dog. Anyhow, I digress. That morning, there were hundreds of people dashing about inside small minibuses, some people heading back to the airport, some people, like us, heading off to the balloon rides. But whatever they were doing, there were lots of them. I'm pretty sure a lot of them didn't realise before that there were two five o'clocks in a day!

Our minibus arrived and we hopped in. We exchanged a 'morning' to the people already on the bus and we were off. We headed out of Goreme and drove for about ten minutes or so. There were minibuses everywhere, even when we seemed to go off road. It was still dark, so we couldn't make anything out, but we eventually stopped on what seemed to be a high grass field. Tea and coffee had been organised already and, as we stepped out of the minibus, we could make out that there were several other minibuses and trailers scattered about on the same field.

It wasn't raining, it wasn't windy, so we were told we had a good chance of flying, but they were all waiting for the signal to go. We had dressed for the occasion, both of us in warm clothing with good footwear. I'd put trousers on and a good flat pair of trainers, thinking back about the videos I'd seen. The sides of the balloon baskets have slots in them on one side, which are the ladders! Then we heard someone shout something and we were good to go. Gulp!

All around us, as the sun was trying to come up, we could hear and see the hot air balloon industry go to work. Balloons were being taken off trailers, men were dashing about everywhere, hot air was being pumped into these massive balloons which were laying on their sides. Men were inside some of the balloon, ropes were being pulled, straighten and attached. It was an amazing site, as wherever you looked there was a balloon being prepared. The noise of the blowers will stay with me forever, it was so exciting to be part of this.

Our balloon was almost ready, and I happened to look over the field, then I wished I hadn't. I saw a fat lady being unceremoniously 'helped' into her basket by two ground crew, they seemed to lift her and thrown her in almost like a sack of potatoes! I took a breath and stepped towards the basket; this was NOT going to happen to me. David stood back to help me, I doubt he knew how scared I was, but probably thought I'd struggle so wanted to help. The basket was rather large and inside it was separated into sections. I set off, putting my feet into the basket steps/slots and was doing OK until I got to the top. I had issues as to where to place my feet to get over the top of the basket. 'Come on Tina, you can do this' was the voice in my head, 'don't make a tit of yourself'. 'You should have been on a diet and lost half your body weight, and then David could have lifted you in. Too late, get in you fat idiot'! In some miraculous way, I was suddenly standing in the basket, no embarrassing potato sack throws, no squeals, no nothing, I had just climbed in. Ha!

David followed me in, way too fit to be in his late fifties, jumping about like a teenager. No justice at all. We were a mixed bunch of people, a lot of Chinese, a couple of Turks, and a couple of French. The pilot was a guy called Memo and he was very good at his job. He firstly explained the position to take when the balloon was landing but he then started lifting the balloon and we all forgot to be scared. The views that were now in front of us were amazing, the sun was fully up and from every surface, there were balloons lifting off the ground. I think it would be amazing to be in a hot air balloon anywhere, but due to the fact that there seemed to be literally hundreds lifting off, it was the most fantastic thing I've ever seen. Different colours, names of businesses, cartoons, every balloon was different.

Memo was constantly on his radio to someone on the ground following us who relayed messages to him, informing him if we could go higher, or if there was a balloon above him and for him to wait. I spoke a little to Memo and he said he'd got the best job in the world. During our travels, David and I have met a few people who think that, but maybe Memo came close to the top of the list.

We continued our flight for some time, maybe an hour, but time just stopped, it was surreal, being above balloons, being below other balloons, travelling across a lunar landscape, with 'fairy chimneys' in the distance and spectacular ground underneath us. Memo then said we would be landing shortly, and I forgot my magical ride and started to think about getting out of the basket. I'd had visions of it landing on its side and being dragged along, I'd had visions of being the last one in the basket and several people needing to be involved with a Hiab to get me out. I had gotten in OK, but oh lord what was heading my way now?

Below, we could see the trailer that had brought the basket to the field we took off from, but why wasn't it being unhooked from the pickup truck? Then we understood why. Memo was landing the basket on the trailer! We couldn't believe it, and he did land it, slap bang on the trailer with just a few inches around it! It was an incredible thing to do as far as we were concerned, but Memo said he did it all the time and didn't think he was doing anything special. That gave me another heart palpitation as I not only had to get out of the basket, but I also had to climb down from the high trailer. Now, if you are a slim woman, you wouldn't worry, you could be lifted off, you could jump like a gazelle, you could fall off and everybody would be concerned. But if you're a fat bird, you'll know my concerns, trying to stay remotely elegant whist at the same time trying hard to get the job done, knowing that if you can't, or that if you fall down, you'll be in zillions of videos with laughter as the sound track!

So without further thinking being involved, I started up the basket slots, there was a member of the ground crew standing on the trailer and he held out his hand, I think he caught the sight of fear in my eyes and smiled, telling me to step onto the hitch of the trailer as I got to the top of the basket, that it would be easier, and it was, he then helped me to climb down from the trailer and I did it with the minimum of fuss and with a little elegance! David hopped out behind me, and then I watched as the other people climbed out, without the help of the nice ground crew member, satisfyingly some of them with no elegance at all. To this day I thank that kind Turkish ground crew man. I think he'd heard me speaking a little Turkish to Memo so took a shine to me a little! But whatever his reason, he helped me to have a fantastic day with David.

The morning wasn't over yet, the crew, once we were all out, opened a bottle or two of something with sparkle and we all had a glass, we were all given an award to say we had undertaken the balloon ride, and we left tips for the fantastic staff. We had a marvellous morning. We were taken back to the hotel and decided it was one of the best things we had done together.

We spent the rest of the day lazing about the hotel pool, a nice meal in the evening and an early night. We had decided to rent a car ready for the next day, and we planned to have a good scout around starting first thing in the morning.

We were up early the next day and had a lovely breakfast on the roof. I discovered that David had been up on the roof at 5am that morning and had taken some great photos of the balloons going over the hotel. We headed off to collect the car and the plan was to visit one of the underground cities. We headed to Derinkuyu, we bought the tickets and headed down, but I'm ashamed to say I was overwhelmed by the tunnels and caves, they were tiny, and I was frightened! We found out later that Kaymakli is the widest, and Derinkuyu, the one we visited, is the deepest. So, if you have any fears of enclosed spaces choose Kaymakli City.

Our next stop was Ihlara Valley. This hadn't been planned, but we had seen the signs for kit, so decided to give it a go. It turns out that it's a valley formed by eruptions and it is a hundred and fifty meters deep and sixteen kilometres long. With a river running along the bottom. The only drawback? Well the only way to the bottom is to walk down three million steps. OK, so I have exaggerated a little, there were only two million! David, God love him, asked if I wanted to do it? I of course thought that I would let him down if I didn't so I said bravely, 'of course I can'. Secretly I was looking at the trees in the bottom of the valley to see how the helicopter would get me out if I collapsed!

We set off down the steps, and if you can imagine, it is a zig zag of steps that are on the valley side, and they take you down to the bottom. It was a lot of steps, but once at the bottom, the valley was pretty easy to walk. We walked alongside the river. Up on the valley sides, there was evidence of human habitation, we were told that there were even churches up on the valley walls. We had walked a few miles when we came to a little oasis. A café perched over the river with seating, tables, and toilets. We stopped for all of the above and had a cold drink. Now this was the time I was starting to think about the steps going back up, planning how I would cope. I'd decided that I'd just climb what I could and then take a photo opportunity stop! Then continue, and repeat. I had realised that maybe there would be a lot of photo stops, but providing I got to the top before the gates of the valley closed then I'd be OK. Wouldn't I?

As we sat drinking, I saw two women, one older and bigger than me talking to one of the staff in the café. They all said bye and the little group walked off away from the café but in the opposite direction of the steps we had come down. A few minutes later, when the café had a quiet moment, I approached one of the guys they had spoken to and asked him about getting out of the valley. He explained that if we kept walking along the way we were going, the valley would suddenly become less steep and that we could walk out, pick up a taxi and they would drive up the steep road back to the car park where we had left our car. That was a result! It was another long walk, but he was right. All of a sudden, we were walking through a gate into a small area with a few shops and cafes.

We beckoned a taxi, jumped in and after a ten-minute taxi ride we were back at the car. I was happy, but I was prepared to climb those steps if I'd had too!

We headed back to Goreme and handed the car back. Tomorrow was our last day, and we planned to visit the Goreme open air museum which was a short taxi ride from the hotel. The last day had arrived and we enjoyed another breakfast on the roof and then headed out to find a taxi, then up to the open-air museum, paid for the ticket and headed in. This museum was full of caves which had been homes, there were churches and sacred places, burial tombs and the most amazing amount of intact structures. It took us a couple of hours to wander around on all the different levels and in and out of all the structures. Back to Goreme and a long relaxing afternoon, including little bit of shopping. Well it would be rude not to. And a nice meal before we went back to the hotel.

The next morning, we were one again up and about at 5am, standing outside waiting for the pick-up for the airport, chatting and listening to our friend the huge lazy dog. Back to the hotel, back through the chaos which was Pegasus check in, a change at Istanbul and then home to the UK and more rain!

If you ever get the opportunity to visit Cappadocia do it. But when you're there do the balloon ride, it's something you will NEVER forget.

A Bulgarian Singer in an Italian Restaurant Run By a Chinese Couple!

I think there's probably only me that could come up with a title for a story like that, but it's the last story in this book and it just has to be done.

At the beginning of 2020 before all the rules came in that changed our lives, we had decided to spend my birthday in Tenerife. My birthday is at the end of February. We both fancied somewhere warm, and I'd looked at the Canaries before as I fancied going away on my own when David was off skiing with his mates, which happens at the beginning of every year. We booked it, and we were winging our way towards Tenerife for a week. A good start, hey?

When the plane reached the Canaries, we started circling. This continued for a fair while, much longer than is usual. It was late evening getting dark when we eventually landed. W very rarely booked package holidays, but this time we had. We went through immigration, got our cases and started looking for our coach. We left the airport and headed outside. The whisper was that we had just landing in a sandstorm which was reason we had been circling around for so long. It seemed OK now though. We climbed onto the coach, the rep popped on for a few seconds then she was gone, and we were off.

We pulled up about 30 minutes later outside a massive hotel. Much bigger than the photos we'd seen. We got off, retrieved our luggage and headed in. The reception, or foyer, or entrance hall, call it what you will, was enormous. It took us a while to even figure out where the reception desk was, but eventually we found it. We checked in, which involved filling in endless forms, and finally we were issued with room number, keys and a MAP of the hotel. We were in. As we crossed the several miles necessary to reach the lifts up to our room, we walked past the light entertainment and their audience. I panicked and said to David 'I'm sorry we can't stay here'. In reply to his question why, I explained I hadn't brough my party frock. Every lady there seemed to have a floral bouncy frock on. Oh my, this wasn't such a good start to a holiday!

The next morning, we were woken by the sound of people shouting. Gallons of water was being run into sinks nearby, and buckets and brushes were being knocked about. We got up and walked out into the hallway. It was actually a fabulous hotel, apart from the frock thing going off downstairs the previous evening. We were in the hallway, but it was actually an open top corridor. The rooms were arranged around a quad, and you could see the floors below. There were flowers and plants everywhere, and from certain points you could see one of the many pools. But this morning, all we could see was sand. Sand everywhere. Sand on every surface, on every floor, sand on all the plants, sand everywhere. During the night the sandstorm had clearly come back.

We found the restaurant and had breakfast and lots of coffee. We headed outside. The pools were all closed. Chairs and loungers were stacked up and the pools were full of sand. It was quite clear to see that each pool had a substantial amount of sand in the bottom. We decided to try our luck beyond the hotel. We walked out of the front of the hotel, and again everything was covered in sand. It was blowing in the wind, and as we walked along the road to where we thought the town centre would be, it was stinging our faces as it blew about. We walked down towards the sea front following the signposts now, and we could see that all of the hotels had the same problem as ours. Swimming pools with sand in their bottom, chairs and loungers pushed into piles. The poor staff were all dashing about just as they had been in our hotel, clearing sand up, moving everything so they could clean and make repairs.

We walked past one hotel and it had a nice Perspex wall. Can you call Perspex a wall? But anyhow it had Perspex all the way around it's boundary. Several pieces of this Perspex had been ripped up and out of their place, so they were now laying smashed and broken on the outside of the hotel boundary. We saw one palm tree that had quite literally been snapped in half. We saw another palm tree that had been ripped up by the roots and smashed through another hotel boundary wall. Devastation was everywhere. The poor shop keepers and bar keepers had opened up, but it was impossible to sit anywhere as they were cleaning up the sand that had been dumped on them.

We walked along the seaside, with the sand still stinging our faces. I had on a pair of sandals with toe posts. They had never bothered me before, but when we got back to the hotel, they had caused massive blisters between my toes. I'm convinced it was sand getting in there! We walked over a bridge and could see people looking down to the road beneath. A lamppost had been ripped up and had gone over the top of the bridge where it had smashed down onto a car. People were standing about around the car, and hopefully no one was injured. But man, oh man, what a shock if you were just driving along and that happened to you.

We spent a lot of that day outside; we found a couple of places that we were able to sit in and get a drink and strangely enough the morale of everyone was good. I supposed they had seen it all before and just got on with it.

That night, even though I didn't have my frock on, we watched a little of the live entertainment before retiring.

The next day was pretty much the same. Although the staff were valiantly fighting the sand, it was still winning, and most of the pools still had a covering on the bottom. We spent time in the town, did a little shopping as I always buy a fridge magnet. That tradition started when my boys, wo are both in the British army, started to travel. I don't mean to Kent or Yorkshire, I mean Kenya and Canada, amongst other fabulous places. They always asked if I wanted anything, so I always asked for a fridge magnet. They were cheap, easily available and take no room to display. Perfect. When David moved in, he works abroad too, so I asked him to do the same. He was amazed. He didn't really know what a fridge magnet was at the time, but then Detroit, Hamburg, Munich, New York, Mexico, Shanghai and lots of other places joined the collection on the fridge door. Over the years, some of my wonderful neighbours, Claire and her family, have brought me them back from their holidays. And of course, David and I get one from every place we visit for the first time together now. So, we have a lot! Anyway, back to my story.

On the third day we were able to grab a lounger by the pool and relax. Its hard work to encourage David to relax, he's normally so busy, and his mind is always on the go. But he is getting better at relaxing, with my help of course. I sat by the pool wondering if I would ever get any of that book that was sitting lurking in my head onto paper. Little did I know that I would have all the time in the world to write it within a month or so. Remember this is the end of February 2020!

That evening we found the most amazing place to eat dinner. We were stopped by a nice young man who 'encouraged' us to go in, which thankfully we did. This place became our go-to restaurant for the rest of our week there. Let me give you a little of the back story here. Earlier that day a hotel about two miles down the road had reported that guests had tested positive for that thing that really stopped 2020 from happening. The poor guests had been locked in. No one was sure what would happen next. Who was to blame? There was lots of gossip, and conjecture was rife.

We walked into this restaurant. It was an Italian restaurant, but there was not one Italian person to be seen. The staff were either Chinese or people born and bred in Tenerife. Or both? We sat and ordered our meal. The staff, all of them, were brilliant! I rarely use that word, being from Yorkshire means that yeah, it's OK is normally the best you'll get. But they were really fantastic. One guy in particular suggested meals and explained what they were. I tried some of the local Tenerife meals and it was fab food. As our meal was being served, a musician had been setting up and this was another wonderful surprise. But probably not for the reasons you'd imagine. He started singing, and it turned out that he was possibly THE worse singer ever! But he was so bad he was bloody fantastic! His 'Thankyaverymuch' at the end of songs done in an Elvis type voice just made David and I love him more. We discovered later that he was Bulgarian. What a random mix we had found, a Bulgarian singer in an Italian restaurant run by Chinese owners!

Not many of those about. We went every night after that, it was so much fun, and the meals were amongst the best I've ever eaten in a restaurant.

One of the days we had whilst in Tenerife, of course had to involve a serious amount of danger. This one was a trip to the Volcano, and of course, the second that David discovered there was a cable car to reach the top of said volcano, we were booked on it! Once again, my nerves of steel were tested. This time however, I was standing next to a little boy of about 11 who was whooping and telling his Mum how great it was. At least I didn't have the stinky armpits or people who had been to Elevenerife. But I couldn't show my fear in front of this little guy, so I stood stoically quietly wishing for the end of this ride to come quicker. I was rather proud of myself!

The rest of the holiday went well. We celebrated my birthday with the Bulgarian singer, but we were still a little worried whether the situation at the hotel down the road would affect us. However, it didn't seem to. We flew back to the UK with no worries.

The next day we went to see my elderly Mum and, as I walked out of the back door she was just collecting her washing from the line. She turned, tripped and fell down. An ambulance was called, and she was taken to the local hospital where it was discovered she had broken her hip. While we were waiting for news about her my phone rang and my boss advised me that I couldn't go to work for the next week. The reason was the problems at the hotel that had been down the road from ours in Tenerife! I had week off work, then ten days back at work, and then, thanks to the bug and the government, enough time off work to write my first book!

That was my last adventure away. Although, I see and do things in a way that is different from most people. So sometimes just a trip to the supermarket is an adventure!

Printed in Great Britain
by Amazon

49996452R00156